The Land the Mind Forgot

The Land the Mind Forgot

Danielle Fiorini

TATE PUBLISHING
AND ENTERPRISES, LLC

Published by Tate Publishing & Enterprises, LLC
127 E. Trade Center Terrace | Mustang, Oklahoma 73064 USA
1.888.361.9473 | www.tatepublishing.com

Tate Publishing is committed to excellence in the publishing industry. The company reflects the philosophy established by the founders, based on Psalm 68:11,
"The Lord gave the word and great was the company of those who published it."

Book design copyright © 2014 by Tate Publishing, LLC. All rights reserved.
Cover design by Christina Hicks
Interior design by Honeylette Pino

Published in the United States of America

ISBN: 978-1-63122-645-8
1. Religion / Christian Life / Personal Growth
2. Religion / Christian Life / Spiritual Growth
14.03.11

The Land the Mind Forgot

Danielle Fiorini

Maria —
you are never
alone!
♡ Dani

Dedication

You have challenged me to find myself, to graciously accept the awkwardness of me. How can I ever repay you? My life turned upside down in a brief second that one snowy day in December. My words to you were, "Everything about your life will change." Guess what? Everything about *my* life changed too. And what a wonderful feeling it is to accept life, celebrate change, and explore dependence. I no longer fear criticism, for you never criticize. *Trust* is no longer an evil five-letter word, for you have never broken my trust, and you have guarded my feelings as if they are your own. When the sun rises in the morning and I prepare for the events of the day, I know things will work out because I know I am loved. I feel loved every moment of the day for you took a moment to listen, not just with your ears but also with your heart. Our hearts speak. We are connected. We are God-centered *best friends*. Thank you! This is just a small celebration of you!

Fractals of You

The beauty of the sunset sinking into the trees
Pales in comparison to the pure heart that I see
The dew on a leaf which magnifies the vein
Quite easily allows me to feel and envelop your pain
A misty morning upon the mountains illuminates a grandeur sky
Before you came, there I sat waiting for life to pass me by
The calmness of the ocean, so placid and so free
Speaks volumes of your trust and honesty

Excitement radiates the sky with colors and amazing light
Our friendship brings laughter and acceptance making my life so bright
The monarch perched so astute, so strong, so bold
I trust you with every fiber of my soul; this you must be told
The moon so distant and so quaint
A fulfilling life of friendship, the picture we will paint
Colorful anemones offer a secure dwelling place
Your open heart coddles my fears, helps me to slow my pace
The crashing of the waves upon the desolate shore
Invite my heart, my soul, my spirit to search and long for more
The trickle of water carries the leaves, the rocks make straight the path
Your unconditional acceptance opens my heart to embrace the daunting tasks
The sun so high in the purple sky emits longing rays so warm
You bring to me the fortitude to break outside the norm
A reflection in a bubble of a life I once had
A gentle hug, a kind word, you pick me up when I am sad
A drip into the water, a ripple into the heart
I know you are always with me even when we are apart
The vibrancy of the morning sun awakens the tired from sleep
All the times that we have shared, these memories I will keep
While some amusement rides bring fun, others bring sheer terror
Much like the times when you tell me to look into the mirror
· The subtle hint of lavender adorns the flower
Prayers with you make me feel empowered
The delicate wings gently come to rest
In all the world, our friendship is the best
Arms outreaching to accept our love and our pain

Our lives come here together, each a sister we have gained
Flip and turn, you now see distortion in an image brand-new
Made from the image that you know, but now with fractals all askew
I see the beauty, the love, compassion, the innocence of you
The twist and the turn, the flip and the wave in totality grew
You bring with you a truth that sets you aside
For you have purest of heart that you just cannot hide
So see these newfound images beauty in and out
For in each is held a truthfulness that one just cannot doubt
And if you cannot see the truth, for the dark has hindered your way
Take this kaleidoscope, your Bible, and pray
For the multitude of images reflect the faith inside
A faith which cultivates, a joy that one cannot hide
For in this joy and love so deep
A friendship, a sisterhood we shall reap.

Contents

Preface

I remember sitting in class as a teenager, innocent and impressionable, as I was asked the question, "Who is God?" Quickly I responded with, "He is one who created us." I carried with me this image of a bearded, elderly man draped in white lines, hovering over a cloud looking down upon earth. This image stayed with me for years because that was the information presented to me.

God loved me and I loved Him, but I was uncertain of the truth of love, the truth of who God was or even who I was in relation to the universe and to God Himself. Nonetheless, I busied myself with the traditional encumbrances, attempting to find myself and put faith first in my life.

My initial calling was to teach, but after several years I moved on in pursuit of other goals and the need to find happiness. I quickly found myself called back to the classroom perplexed for I had not yet found the sought-after happiness. Blindly, I followed my heart, not knowing where it would lead.

Little did I know that my first few steps back into the classroom would become the greatest steps of my life, for these became the steps which deepened my understanding that faith need not be a daily struggle for dominance; rather, faith need be my lifestyle.

Classroom discussions with my students brought clarification to my faith exploration, which further led to deep meditations of my life connection with God. In the classroom, I sat, paging through textbook after textbook, preparing lessons that would captivate the students. In my preparations, my heart opened and the words of the pages filled my soul that I learned to live the love of my heart.

Questions arose and I found my responses enlightened, clarified by faith. Discussions brewed, arguments tempered; yet with each, a manifestation of love, God's love. It was not until a discussion of man-created morality did the notion of God reality or wordless words surface. Life, as I learned from introspective faith education coupled with innate knowledge, is a choice to defy a rational mind or a choice to embrace the rational mind. Life, then, is the duality of faith versus thesis.

When posed with the question of what God was doing before he created the world, St. Augustine responded with, "Nothing, He didn't have the time."

What a powerful statement!

Humans conceived this measurement to create an illusion of normalcy, thus fabricating an understanding of an otherwise unknown. But what have we created: deadlines, lateness, exhaustion? We seem to always be praying for more time, just a little more time. In our attempt to rationalize our world, we have segregated ourselves from the divine. Our life of faith is no longer a love story but rather an arduous expedition, a search to find God and know God. Though God is ever present, we often find it difficult to sift through logical thought, to stop and discover our hearts, and therefore our connection with God. It is much easier to blindly follow a secular lifestyle when these falsehoods lay a solid foundation of denial and preposterous theories supposedly proven by fact and intelligence.

Society has instilled in us this plausible idea that our job is to analyze, debate, and prove. How can we prove God? Quite simply, look around. Look at the beauty, perplexity, and reality that is creation. From the fact that a bee defies our scientific concepts in its flight to the entire process of human conception, God has formed creation in all its glory and majesty. It is only when we stop and listen, not with our ears but with our hearts, do we begin to feel a love story as was God's original intention. In a world devoid of morals, we are charged with becoming the epitome of faith. How do we do this? We love, we feel, we experience with our hearts. This approach to life will bring with it our share of alienation, heartache, even trauma. If we are honest, it is with each lonely night, with each hurtful comment, with the death of a loved one that transforms us into the person we are today. As each piece of our life's puzzle is intricately placed, we begin to see the whole picture. We are not alone; that which was created for us by God is all we need to thrive in this world if only we are able to let go of human theories carved into the mind like an engraver carves into stone. Only the theories posed by the mind can quickly be erased and altered once the heart is heard unlike that of chiseled stone. The journey of our world, the journey to our world begins with a pause, a listen, and an acknowledgment of the heart. How does the heart speak?

This book is a simple guide to help us reconnect to the heart, to fuse together our soul with the soul of God. Take each section in stride, pause, and listen to the heart for it is in truth of self that we find acceptance, love, and the grace of God dwelling within our very soul. We can learn to be real, to be the love God promises, but to do this, we must feel, we must live, we must listen to the wordless words of the heart, for they speak the truth of God… God's love for us, echoing in our very soul.

The question remains how does the heart speak? Yet more importantly, how do we listen to the heart? Use this book to trace your journey, your faith journey, your love story with a God whose unconditional love is unmatched yet readily available. Take your time, maybe journal or sketch, but do not fear discovery for the discovery of a God-reliant world is a world filled with love, filled with joy, filled with peace even when life itself falls among the thorns. Settle into your heart, God speaks. If at first a whisper, listen until you uncover God in truth, God in love, God in you. Settle into your heart and listen.

The rain vehemently falls, and the ground becomes super saturated, repelling the water. As the surface water collects and the wind howls, the ground becomes slick making for treacherous walking conditions. Hearing the rain and the wind whip around, we prepare ourselves for the day with warm clothing, boots, and an umbrella. Raw emotion is just like the rain, for though we don't want it, and we cannot control it, we must forge ahead through it. Equipped with knowledge, prayer, and unconditional love, we trek into the cold rain somewhat protected until the wind whips through our very soul leaving us exposed and vulnerable. Rational, logical thought ridicules our God connection, leaving us feeling naked for the world to mock and jeer. Instinctually, we want to run and hide, climb back into bed, pull the covers over our heads, and pretend the day never began. Yet we remain standing in a puddle, cold and wet, though we do not melt. Raw emotion is the most powerful of all emotions, as it is real and not easily understood; it comes out of the blue and attacks at the most inopportune time. But it is what we do with this emotion that makes the difference. Just as we cannot control the rain, we should not attempt to control the raw emotions, which surface from our heart. Rationalizing raw emotion brings with it feelings of incompetence, frustration, and aggravation, feelings which inhibit our heart from leading us through the day. Remembering our umbrella on that rainy day, we now open it. Sheltered from logical thought our heart begins to lead as unconditional acceptance, unconditional love, and unconditional patience fall from the open umbrella. Permanently fortified in God, we make our way through the rain no longer crippled by raw emotion for we understand that emotions will come and go, and they need not be rationally explained. They may hamper us for a bit. But, we have the choice to run back inside or open our own umbrella. Our choice to remain in the rain allows us to grow, for as the umbrella opens, so too, our heart opens and begins to gently take the lead in our life. Our heart, our soul, is God within us; thus, with God leading our journey, we are always protected from negative elements and though we may get a little cold and wet at times we will not freeze nor melt. The love of God will remain the fire which warms and the umbrella which shelters; shelters our most vulnerable of emotions. As the rains subside and the winds die, a rainbow appears as a sign of peace, a sign of a restful soul. Let us learn to rest our soul in the arms of God.

Epic Battle, the Heart the Victor

Epic Battle, the Heart the Victor

We are human: we live, we breathe, we make mistakes, we hurt, and we hurt others. We carry with us emotions of anger, hatred, jealousy, and we crumble with feelings of unconditional love, acceptance and patience. Why would God live in us, how would God live in us, and where would God live in us? I can recall the childhood banter of, "I know who you are but who am I?" As children, we would never respond with, "I am a child of God and He lives in me". We would have been laughed off the playground. But aren't we just that, God's children and His dwelling place?

As humans, we find it difficult to comprehend God. Our relation to a deity that has no beginning or end is so perplexing, so unreal, because it is far beyond our intellectual grasp. Yet we were given the person of Jesus, God among us, God with us. As humans, we are physically strong-armed by that which we do not understand for our societal status is often based upon knowledge and analysis of logic. God repudiates reason and logic, for our creation was deliberate love and affection. Intrinsically, our goodness shines forth, for we are made in the image and likeness of God; we have a God connection. We carry with us Godly traits, yet we do not possess them to the fullest as does God. How do we know which traits to foster and which traits to save for later? Simply put, God.

God, the lifeblood of the soul, resides within us in our every move, every thought, every action. Our upbringing, however, teaches that honor, glory, and strength are products of self-promotion, self-determination—in a sense, pride. Vain glory detracts from the soul, for it discounts our dependence upon God, the God reliance and relationship as intended upon creation. Scientific studies, theorems, graduate research, and proofs through analysis can only take us so far. God must take us the rest of the way. But if we spend our lives in the here and now, how do we recognize God? If everything can be explained rationally and God defies logic, where does that leave God?

For some, God is a figment of the imagination concocted on a whim to ease the minds of restless beings that need to fill a void in their lives. For others, *God* is a term used to denote a deity, something larger than life itself, a tool used to correct any error in the findings of scientific data. For the faith-filled believer, God is a partner in an otherwise cold, cruel world, who understands pain and wants to heal, who understands fear and wants to be our safety net, who understands desperation and wants to be comfort. God understands our human insecurities; however, do we respond to his invitation to be our confidant, our truth, our treasured friend? It is God who understands love and puts no conditions upon it, who understands joy as a heartfelt leap which ignites life within the very soul, who understands freedom for he has given us free will. It is in our freedom that we are able to find God dwelling in the very depth of our soul. God told us that we are temples of the Holy Spirit, the third person of the Trinity, given to us to help and guide throughout life's trials and tribulations. We have also been told that God dwells in his holy temple. So if we are the temple of the Holy Spirit and God dwells within his temple and the Holy Spirit is God, then God must live in us. If God lives in us and God is good, then we are inherently good. We are deserving of love, forgiveness, and peace. The joy we desire will be found when our "God connection" is restored

and manifested in love. A subservient mind leads to an unbiased heart, which finds its path, lit by humility, faith and desire, to God.

How do we quiet our logical thoughts so as to recognize God? While we can identify God through our senses, it is the notion of the sixth sense that brings God to fruition. We feel God's presence upon the acceptance of a hug from a loved one or best friend. We hear God's voice as the wind gently tickles the leaves, which have chosen to remain on the winter-stricken trees. We hear God's laughter as a child retells a joke that was invented on the playground but is only understood in the mind of a six-year-old. We see God in the magnificent luminaries of the sky, the rays of the sun by day, and the wondrous stars by night. Yet it is in our genuine openness to God that these senses are taken to new heights and seen for what they are, God visible in a reason driven world. We invite God to be our companion in our life journey, for we gain strength from God, not independent of God. We recognize what we know. If we recognize beauty, then we are beauty. If we recognize love, then we are love. If we recognize peace, then we are peace.

That is not to say that we emulate every aspect of beauty, love, or peace, but we have seen it. In some aspects, we have felt it, and we have experienced it. If we have never seen a pen, then we could not recognize it as such. Since our perception is reality, then understanding and recognition comes from within and is not reliant upon outside factors, false perceptions, or definitions. Therefore, we recognize God as we have an intimate knowledge and understanding of God because God resides within our very soul. The feeling of steadfast love, the feeling of humble grace is the presence of God within us—our beautiful soul, our pure heart, our reflected image in the mirror. Should this vision be our heart's desire, then we must look, stare, and ponder for the heart's competition with the mind can prove to be an epic battle, a battle sure to leave scars but worth each wound incurred. And so we must look deep within, evaluate our worth and proceed with caution, for life has some wicked turns, detours, and even closed roads. While our ride may be mapped out, we need to be ready to journey the uncharted roads. This openness will enable joy to be the root of our lives, even in the midst of turmoil.

At the request of my best friend, I was asked to look into the mirror and report back my findings. This is an exercise I had suggested to her that she may see the pure heart I readily saw with each interaction with her. The tables were now turned on me. I found the exercise difficult. With each initial look, I looked away. I did not know what I feared. Maybe I feared truth. Maybe I feared fabricated theses contrived by the human spirit; regardless, I looked away. As I prompted my best friend, "Just look, think nothing and just feel", these words quickly haunted me as they came through illuminating my cell phone screen with each text. And so I listened. I thought nothing and just looked. It was in a moment of complete silence that I saw, for the first time, a beautiful soul. I saw not my eyes, but the eyes of God staring back at me in the mirror. Tears streamed down my face, for all the words I had spoken, repeating what I was taught and believed, now became my reality; God was inside of me...living within me!

We live in a world plagued by righteousness, infested with pride, and saturated in doubt, surviving alone (for dependence is for suckers), we learn to stonewall our every action, our every thought, that we may be protected from criticism hiding just around the corner. Life quickly swallowed, the abyss widens, gapping even the minute knowledge and understanding of self. Monotonous undertakings monopolize the mind, and the heart is lost. An island unto ourselves, we reiterate the proverbial phrase, "I am strong. I do not need anyone."

Life's mantra pains, it cuts for tears are shed in the silence of the night, and words of the heart are spoken, even hopelessly screamed for the mind holds us prisoner. Shackled by logic, the heart caged like a wild animal longing to be freed, longing to explore, longing to live as God intended, free and loved. Scratched and scared from the tugging, the pulling, the frantic flailing to be freed from the treacherous torments ensued by the mind, the body weakens, our fight flounders, our voice is deemed lost. Traveling down the same paths, the familiarity is anything but a comfort. It antagonizes, jeers, and mocks with each passing. The heart quickly encases in stone for protection, that it might not become bruised and tattered like the body. The layers grow thicker, almost impenetrable. Ah, protection the succulent decoy mischievously baited by the mind. Fabricated realities lurk in the shadows, which, when brought into the light, are nothing more than absurd breaches of truth romantically delineated by a magnanimous deviant—the mind.

Sucked in, the mind quarterbacks our every action, and life becomes hollow. We become a shell of a being; even a light breeze warrants fear of an adversary. Choices perpetually bombard the heart, choices which are dauntingly leashed by logical expressions of truth, yet truth the hidden gem.

Fear, logic, irrational feelings, and sadness: all validations of the walls built around the heart, protection of the truth from within. Calloused, we hesitantly tread life's lonely path in an effort to find that which our heart so desperately desires—unconditional love. Step by step, the melancholic journey becomes so mundane, so stifling that goals and desires are thrown by the wayside as we gallantly search for an opening, a crack, a crumbling stone in the mending wall thought to be the protector of our heart. The journey becomes tiresome, we grow weary for we believe our efforts to be in vain as even the sun's rays could not penetrate the thickness of the forest. The cold air chills our soul, and we begin to walk in circles, aimlessly wandering, our purpose forgotten. Time passes, the darkness seems to thicken, the treads of shoes worn so thin we begin to feel the pain of each pebble we step upon. The thinning of the sole is just a metaphor for the weaning of our soul, our hope, our drive to find and nourish our God connection. As our emotional struggle begins to debilitate, our strides shorten, our steps slow. The sights and sounds of the forest begin to frighten. Paralyzed with fear, the question runs rampant in our mind—run or hide? The darkness encompasses, and the mighty evergreen trees begin casting shadows, imposing fright, and terrifying the soul. Encapsulated in fear, we run to escape the noise, which has become so deafening, so perplexing, so painful. Stride for stride, the noise continues to permeate the forest, we lose our footing, and we find ourselves face down in a pond. The troubled water reflects a startling image, one that was thought to be lost in the travels of the forest; yet familiar, gentle, compassionate eyes stare back as the waters settle. The tepid water warms not only our physical being, but warms the heart which begins to feel again. Rejuvenated, the journey to find a break in the wall recommences. With a kick in our step and warmth in our heart, we believe this miraculous pond to be the fountain of youth. Folklore, the fountain of youth does not exist; why then is fear and anxiety replaced by fortitude and peace? Ah, the pond was a magical pond, indeed, for its reflection was that of the soul, the very "God connect" we were in search of from the onset.

Our mind becomes clear, the perceived darkness was nothing more than our eyes closed in fear and the cold that shook our very core, perceived as painful weathering of the elements, was nothing more the spirit of God carrying us to safety. The monotonous walk through the thickets and brush necessitated the need for our introspection; true, it was coupled with doubt and trepidation, but it was in questioning that we found answers. The perceived eerie sounds echoing throughout the forest were simply the voice of God reverberating from the hollow caverns of our soul. The echoing voice continued, and because it was unrecognizable, it was deemed a threat; thus, flight was our answer. The rustling of the bushes which initially caused temporary paralysis was God's answer to our strongest desire—a shared life in love. The ego forcefully and defiantly misrepresents life events, situations, and communications thus impeding our relationship with God and our longing for love. It was not until we were brought to the pond and waded in the water long enough to siphon through our "God connect" clues that we understood God's dwelling is not only within each of us but in all that the sun touches. Our duty is to identify God and to communicate with God. To do this, we must set aside our logical, human mind and learn to communicate with our heart. Communication with the heart invites confidence, trust, understanding, and truth all which require us to step out from the shadows of the evergreen and be touched by the light, the love of God dwelling in the depths of our soul yet concealed by protective walls. The walls must be expunged, but the mortar of the mind has interwoven steel bars reinforcing the strength of each brick.

Have you ever found yourself wandering from place to place not knowing what you were looking for or if you were even moving in the right direction? When I went off to college, I thought to myself, "Great, now I can reinvent me, the me I could never seem to be." I had chosen a college far from home, one in which no one from my high school was attending so I thought it was a perfect time to create this new me. It did not happen. The masks were too many, the wall around my heart was too thick.

Each attempt to venture into the foreign land of self discovery only created another masked layer. So college continued with faith in my heart and blinders disguising the reality of God in my midst. Though I continued to fight for the dominance of faith, I wanted so badly to discover the God of my heart, the words of my soul. I wrote, I prayed,

I attended church services all in the hopes to discover change and to uncover the truth of my heart, God. After college, I found a job teaching and though I loved my job, I never felt whole. So I left in pursuit of wholeness, of completeness. I found another teaching job closer to home and thought, "That is what was missing. I was too far from home". That was not the case. I was teaching and coaching, two things I loved, I was close to home and had a great apartment and yet I was lonely, lost. I knew God loved me, I knew God was in all that I could see yet I could not feel this love for I knew love only via description not interaction.

Still chomping at the bit, I wanted, no I needed to feel alive, to feel love, to feel connected, emotionally, with God. In the short period of seven years, I had lived in six different cities, all were an attempt to discover me or to reinvent me, all attempts were met with opposition either self-inflicted or permissibly inflicted by others; failure was my victor's cup. It was not until faced with the impending death of my mother, of which I will get into later, did my faith become my person and I was able to allow my heart to circumnavigate the mind and place the words of love into my soul. I heard, for the first time the truth of my heart, the truth of God's presence speak and it had my voice.

The heart speaks, and the ears strain to hear, for the mortar and bricks muffle the calling of God. These words need not be heard with our ears, for they are felt with ever fiber of our being yet in is incumbent upon us to stop, listen, and believe that which the heart speaks. Life keeps us moving, looking in new directions, revisiting the past, yet how often do we stop and truly listen, truly settle the mind that the soul may speak and honestly be heard? Imparting of wisdom is God's greatest gift, for it is wisdom that reveals God in our hearts, reveals

God in our relationships, reveals God in our experiences, reveals God's unconditional love extemporaneously present in all the accords of life.

Stop, listen, believe the words of the heart, wordless words, echoing in the soul, circumventing the mind, causing the mortar to crumble. As the mortar crumbles, the bricks loosen and sound begins to penetrate, echoing from the caverns of the soul. The mind slows, and so it begins to listen. Introspective thoughts run rampant, systematically blocking the logical thoughts which impede upon the feelings of the heart. As questions continue to bombard, the heart takes the reigns, humility its path, patience its course, and openness the lights along the path. The "wordless words" spoken from the heart are finally heard by the mind:

What do you need right now? What do you need to hear? That I love because I do. That I will always accept you, I will. That I put no conditions upon our relationship, because I don't. That I am proud of you, because I am. That our conversations are times that I cherish, because I do. That you are so special to me, because you are. That you have a pure heart, because you do. That you use your gifts to help others, because you do. That you are genuinely good and loving, because you are. That you are stronger than you know, because you are. That you can always trust me, because you can. That you are always on my mind, because you are. That when you smile, I smile, because I do. That my love is for you, because it is. That I will harbor your pain, because I will. That I will honor your person, because I do. That your tears bring tears to my eyes, because they do. That you are wonderful, because you are.

What do you need to believe? What do you need to feel? That your faith has carried you, because it has. That peace will find you, because it will. That fortitude strengthens your step, because it does. That joy will envelop you, because it will. That understanding has enriched your life, because it has. That your kindness does not go unnoticed, because it doesn't. That your tenderness brings comfort, because it does. That your honesty can be seen in your eyes, because it can. That your dedication to friendship is commendable, because it is. That your laughter fills my heart with smiles, because it does. That your honesty warms my heart, because it does.

Do you know that you deserve: love, to feel safe, to trust, to be trusted, to be you, to wake up every morning with a smile on your face and warmth in your heart, to never be judged, to enjoy life, to feel, to live, to be loved, friendship, peace, joy, to cry, to scream; all without conditions?

I will walk with you, I will carry you, I will listen to you, I will celebrate you. You are my child and I love you. You are so very special to me. Please listen to my words, feel them, live them. I am with you always.

Love,
God

The words of God are the key to the lock on the cage, yet how do we make it fit? Do we turn the key in the proper direction? Do we even realize that the key has been found? When we consider life's actions to be a purposeful misguiding of the mind, the persistent melody of the heart produces the overture of the soul. The notes no longer complacently reside upon the diatonic scale; rather, the notes anxiously await a new placement that an innovative melody may be performed. A change from a treble clef to a bass clef and the song transforms, and it takes on a new identity. Identifying with our souls, who we are, our future path as determined by our now, becomes a daunting task for our transformation connects not only with our worth but with our understanding of our worth, our perception of love, our understanding of love, and our willingness to change morphed into that which we are, the dwelling place of God. Throughout life we change, we develop, we change again, we search, we change, we pray, we talk, we change, we love, we grow, and we live. The reality of life lived comes with the realization that the mind perplexes, it banes, and to break free from this false existence, we must look deep within our soul, step outside our comfort zone, experience and embrace change, "God change." God change, found in the depths of our soul, is sought and discovered by silent communication, respectful perception, sense awareness, and truthful introspection, otherwise known as prayer.

Identity Uncovered

Identity Uncovered

A metamorphosis of life

A small, white, oval egg is found on a leaf, exposed to the elements of nature. It looks defenseless, yet it clings onto the leaf. In approximately four days, a caterpillar will emerge, hungry for food. The only job of this tiny caterpillar is to eat and to grow. In two weeks' time, this caterpillar will be eating every leafy green in its path as it seeks nutrients, which promote growth. Unlike other creatures, the skin of a caterpillar does not expand; rather, in a short time, the skin is shed allowing for the caterpillar to grow. This process occurs four times in the brief life cycle of a caterpillar. When the caterpillar has eaten enough, a chrysalis is formed; and for ten days, this insect is nestled in a protective enclave. The growth process continues until a beautiful butterfly emerges ready to live its life and soar with the winds, embracing each moment of grandeur. Our lives are much like the life cycle of a monarch butterfly, as we too experience a metamorphosis. Born

completely free, innocent of societal pressures and norms, we believe what we see, we know what we have been taught, and we live what we have experienced. Just as the tiny caterpillar munches on the leafy greens, we ingest every word spoken, every hug embraced, every lie told, every tear shed, every door slammed, every knee bent in prayer. Life continues and we watch, we absorb life experience, though many never see us watching. As we mature, we question; some are vocalize, and some lie in the silence of our hearts. It is here that we find answers, be they completely bogus, misguided, or conversely enlightening and sculpting. They are answers that nonetheless shape our lives. Like the caterpillar, we shed, not skin, but personalities. We toil with ways to better adapt to our surroundings, for it is here that we want to please and become part of he popular crowd, thus shedding that which causes mockery and painful jest. This process continues, and with it come walls of protection, that the innocent child may not be hurt; thus, the walls are erected in an effort to dull the pain and bring happiness.

Before we know it, a huge chrysalis is formed around us. We can see out, but no one can penetrate the walls of this chrysalis, for they have become our protection. Operating our lives from within this clear protective covering proves challenging, but we are strong, we are survivors, we need no one, so we independently find a way to make life work... We find happiness. Looking at life through a clear, protective shell creates a warped sense of reality, for the light entering into the chrysalis is refracted, not reflected. It is with the bending of this light that we become complacent and duped, for life is not being lived, rather than masqueraded under false pretenses and guises, which are mere fabrications of reality. Understanding, wisdom, and faith can penetrate this chrysalis, providing clarity. This certainty and Godly strength smolders within us, and as we embrace these gifts, they multiply. Enlightenment of the mind enables us to see God, to see our worth, to embrace the necessary changes and find a reflection of self, magnified in love. It is with eyes wide that we begin to see life; we begin to experience life not in the seclusion of self, the seclusion of the chrysalis, though this still remains for a time. We now see that happiness is an illusion that independence can be synonymous with loneliness, that strength exists only in God, and life is meant to be shared, not kept to ourselves. A metamorphosis occurs, our wings develop, and we shed the last bit of protection for we no longer need to be protected. As we emerge from the chrysalis, life looks different. Everything looks greener, brighter, our path clearer, and the air soothes the jumpy nerves as we take flight for the first time. Just as the butterfly opens its wings and makes its momentous first flight, we too are empowered by God to take flight and live life. Our beauty is mesmerizing for we are love, we are truth, we are free to be, we are joy, and we are peace, for it has been lying within our souls since birth. Discovery has proven worthy as life now begins, life in the arms of God. Cleansed by this truthful discovery, our eyes are opened, our heart awakened, and our mind becomes timid, enabling us to recognize and accept beauty, our beauty. Judgments offset by love, choices empowered by dependence, understanding experienced in freedom; the wordless words become a familiar companion. A mesmerizing voice, a comforting feeling, a vivid aspiration, God's love becomes paramount, and the mind retreats that life may be enjoyed in the beauty of nature such as a snowstorm.

The beauty of a snowfall begins to warm the soul with tender resignation to innocence and solace. Each flake which falls from the sky is an image, a snapshot, of the uniqueness of God. The uniqueness of each snowflake developing as crystallization occurs mimics the individuality of the human soul. Superficially, our logical thoughts may echo each other; yet it is in our spiritual dwelling that we differ. God within us; soul ignited in love, desiring truth, hoping in joy, reverent in wisdom and persevering in faith. Why do some people love without worry and others stress and fret? Why are some people always prepared while others frantically scour the land for happiness? The knapsack some so effortlessly throw over their shoulder acts as a millstone weighing others down to the point of exhaustion. The tools inside are the same so why such a polar response to its weight? Some choose to labor with a screwdriver when it would be easier to use a drill. Such is the case with the knapsack, for if we know what is inside the bag and have confidence in our ability to use the tools, the weight is of no concern. The converse is also true. Should we lack confidence in our judgment to use the correct tool or our ability to use the chosen tool to its fullest potential, then that weight of the bag is bothersome and as we drag it around we become obstinate, even resentful, that we must endure the weight of such a useless bag. What we fail to recognize is that the knapsack is like no other knapsack in that it is our gift from God; the tools previously under the logical guise of a hammer, wrench, crowbar, and drill begin to create a new silhouette. No longer familiar to the rational eye, an overwhelming feeling emerges as the soul takes flight, leading with the heart to be schooled in each tool of the soul. Faith affords us the familiarity to unzip the knapsack and discover what we have been carrying around for years. Fortitude, the hammer of the heart, pounds into us the courage to overcome adversity. Wisdom allows us to adjust to our surroundings, opening our eyes to the vision of God, the protection of God, the presence of God in our lives. Prying away that which inhibits us from fully comprehending God's revelation in our lives, we become blessed with the gift of understanding. It is in this understanding of God's promise and fulfillment of the promise that the crowbar is tossed aside and the drill sought. Humility fits this tool well as screws are deeply drilled or gently removed. Humility allows us to dig deep, assert Godly pressure, pull back or out when necessary, expect no recognition and move forward. We find that as we learn the use and limit of every tool, our confidence is strengthened, and we take ownership of the craftsmanship and ability of each tool. Funny, those who laboriously carry their bag throughout life are the ones who have never unzipped the bag and therefore weigh the contents as foreign and awkward.

I was one of these people who carried the bag. Sure I may have peeked in, deemed the contents as foreign and quickly shut the bag. I thought, "Well, at least I have the bag. That should do some good." I carried it with me, ever cognizant of its weight hoping the contents would one day would be revealed to me in an epiphany and that somehow I would be infused with the knowledge and understanding of each tool. Never did I think that I would have to actively learn the tools of the bag. But there I was, a new mother unsure of how to even change a diaper let alone raise a child and I found myself holding my own mother's hand, preparing her for her death. There was so much I wanted to say, so much I wanted to do but I fell mute. In college I had had some classes in death and dying, I understood the human process, the stages of death by Kubler Ross; but this, this was a spiritual experience. This was life, the truth of life, the truth of our connection with our eternal God. Though faith was never common talk at my dinner table, faith was elevated to a Godly nature and treated with the upmost respect. Faith and God are what carried me through those two months as I told my mom to take her (deceased) father's hand and be free of her physical ailments. She eventually went to her eternal rest and only then did I realize that I had opened my sack and learned to how to use its contents. From that moment on, I fully understood that life was mine to embrace. I took charge of my person, and began to walk in faith, knowing I had all I needed for my journey in my knapsack.

Those who have invested time, love, and interest into the proper use of each tool have an abundance of tools and carry the knapsack as though it were the weight of a feather. Love, live, preserve, thrive, praise, hope, run free—these are the lessons of the tools found within the knapsack. Live with God, live in love, and live in acceptance.

Wipe away the glistening snowflakes that have accumulated on the unattended knapsack, and there we find a uniqueness unlike any other—a uniqueness coupled with God and God tools. Will you be schooled in these God tools or will you let them rust in the new fallen snow?

Maredith Free

Intimate Connection. Connecting Intimately

Intimate Connection, Connecting Intimately

Awkward pauses and awkward thoughts can bring about awkward realizations yet awakenings, for they revive the heart, perpetuate the voice of the soul, and propel the mind to disregard the fabricated love which surrounds our every day experiences. Barefaced conversations of the heart permeate through the soul, and the mind listens. It hears the truth for the first time. It understands the shallow, superficial workings of societal norms, which consistently disregard the tender "wordless words" of God. Understanding, love, and faith are all forerunners of these words, for with each embrace a mask, worn as armor to safeguard the heart, disappears to reveal that the heart itself is the protection; the masks serves only as a covering.

I spent years wandering through life, blindly following the validated doctrines of Christianity though never completely understanding said beliefs. Life was black and white, there were no shades of gray for it either fit or it didn't, it was that simple. As a child, I was introverted, to say the least, and I just absorbed my surroundings. I kept my thoughts to myself for it seemed that any time I ventured to share my thoughts I was mocked or ridiculed by friends and family so it was easier just to remain silent. If I were forced to talk, I spoke with deliberate words so as not to be laughed at for the scars of my youth still raw with pain. With each interaction came an understanding of the need to protect the heart. I had confused my pain with that of emotional stress, therefore the need to feel was overrated as it brought with it pain and heartache; neither of which I wanted in my life. Robotic in thought yet life-like in movement, my life became a shell of the human mind, a drone of its existence. With the passing of my mother, I came to understand the purpose of the heart, the reason and need for feelings. In not allowing the bad to enter, I also kept the good at bay, and kept love at arm's length. I discovered my heart. I heard the wordless words as God spoke to me and, for the first time, I listened.

A crowded market is alive with miserable people frantically grabbing items from the shelf, throwing them into their carts, impatiently waiting at the checkout, then rushing to their cars to return home, only to wait. Surveying the barren shelves we find that the bread, milk, and eggs have all been depleted. Ah, a storm must be approaching, thus explaining the testy attitudes of the shoppers who needed to get supplies to make French toast, should they be stuck inside their homes for a couple of days. The market is not the only place inundated with misery, as the wait in line at the gas station becomes increasingly hostile. Arguments ensue when cars are left abandoned at the pump while their owners rush inside to get the last bag of rock salt and a shovel. Individuals choose to weather each storm differently, but for most, it often brings to light a sense of vulnerability, a lack of preparedness, or a feeling of fear of the unknown.

Often viewed as a storm, life carries with it many uncertainties. These unknowns frighten, even petrify, for if we are caught off guard, we may become exposed as imperfect beings. To ensure this inferior person is not exposed, we create walls around our frailties. Though these walls are erected to protect, their purpose becomes skewed when self-recognition is no longer possible. In an attempt to deflect feelings of vulnerability and lack of conformity, we wear masks and, in essence, become who others want us to be. This act of leaving behind our true self hardens our heart and distracts our mind, forcing aspects of our person to become hidden. Just as people frantically prepare for the storm with last-minute shopping, we frantically look for our true self. Sheepishly putting together socially accepted ingredients, we fabricate that which others define as acceptable, becoming carbon copies, transient vagrants hopelessly wandering in search of independence, freedom, and permission to think, feel, and live a life of love. Just as the snow accumulates and we hesitantly look to our provisions questioning whether our preparations were enough to weather the storm, so too we look to our hearts only to find loneliness, hurt, and fear. In an effort to deflect such raw emotion, we put in place another mask and forge on with a smile and French toast in hand. Resentment and even anger build as storm after storm, we rush to the market for last minute provisions fully aware that there are people who have no need to last minute shop or fill their tanks. These people do not anxiously await the arrival of the storm. Instead, the placidly go about their business and deal with the elements of the storm upon arrival. Thinking life too complicated, we choose to go about our business surviving instead of thriving. God speaks, how do we listen? Do we hear the wordless words eloquently spoken, genuinely offered through God's gracious gift of unconditional love? Prayer is our source of self-recognition, identification, and rediscovered vigor for life itself.

Life found silence profound for God abounds in life itself. Prayer connects and reconciles our heart with life: love, the anesthesia awaiting breath. The breath of life, the breath of love fills the heart, the mind succumbs to the power of the wordless words clearly articulated in the caverns of the soul, painted in the landscapes of wonder and enveloped in the embrace of a trusted friend. Nestled, warm, cozy, loved, yet paralyzed with fear, for the mere thought of movement is equated with the loss of the feeling of security. Alas, the new morning sun rises, obligations must be met, careers placated, and life explored independent of the physical; thus, the day begins. As the day unfolds, there are isolated moments of peace and tranquility, moments in which the heart journeys to the place of warmth and comfort experienced in the early morning meditation. Plagued by a question, "How can the love and tenderness so strongly encountered in the isolation of the morning slumber genuinely be felt among the chaotic, insincerities experienced among the apathetic majority dwelling within the urban jungle?" An epiphany hits like a Mack truck—God. Selfishly thinking that happiness and strength came solely from within, independent of God, it was concluded that love came from interactions with others; thus, when others were filled with negativity and hatred, love could not be present or felt. This erroneous conclusion was brought to light through the power of prayer.

I was indeed humbled by these findings. A retreat of prayerful contemplation uncovered intriguing answers that stimulate the soul, invigorate the spirit, and entice introspection. God has provided us the tools to thrive in this world, not just survive. A product of survival for so long the assumption was made that life was about survival not about fulfillment. Seeking, longing, wanting, searching for that blissful feeling to return and envelop all the causes of pain, of hurt, of mistrust, a prayerful plea was made and heard. As one prays, concerns are readily spoken and quickly forgotten by the sender. The request heard, the request answered, yet the intended recipient consumed with life forgets to stop, listen, and believe that which is spoken in the silence of the heart. Time expires. A weary, heavy heart surrenders to the contests of the mind, the reply scrambled by logic, the message never received. Life continues, shallow interactions overwhelm the spirit, and once again, prayer is the fall back. When will we stop? How will we listen? What must we believe? The mind fools us into believing that God does not exist for he did not answer our prayer. Prayer is not a magic eight ball. It is not a child's Christmas wish list. It is our open communication: talking to, listening to, witnessing God in our lives. And so we stop, we listen, and we believe… Invested in prayer is to be enveloped in love, unconditional love, which prompts the soul to guide and speak. What do we truly know?

As the sun breaks through the dark clouds, the night loosens its monopoly on the sky, and day dawns. The rays shine upon the earth with a tender force, the water glistens, the trees rustle in the gentle breeze, and the heart is warmed by the knowledge that God drives this dawning. The day mimics the heart's connection to God. God speaks with intensity reiterating his promise of unconditional love. Life is love, and the dawn speaks of such love. The vibrant colors of the sky warm the heart. It beats with certainty. It awakens, not in haste, but rather in peace for the invitation to wake in the arms of God is accepted. The cool breeze that gently tickles the leaves now tenderly caresses the cheeks—a kiss from God. As the morning continues to unfold, the sun kisses each flower that it may slowly awaken, adding to the intensity of love with its fervent hues adorning the hillsides and valleys. The waters move with precision, glistening in the rays of the sun, as if to say, "I am love flowing for all to see." The birds dance, silhouetting love against the glow of the magnificent sun. Shaping in love, the grandeur of the day awaits, the promise of love, a reality in sight. Preparations for the day continue, saturated in love.

Each step taken is taken in love, each breath is breathed in love, and each word spoken is spoken in love, for life is love, and love is real. Eyes are open to see, ears are open to hear, the heart is free to feel the love set before us in the light of our surroundings. The door shuts and work becomes the plausible reality as the mind slowly penetrates the heart until it completely infiltrates the spirit becoming the antithesis of the heart. Deadlines, coupled with anxiety, occupy the day. A quick glance at the clock and a resounding jubilation comes from the cubicles. The work site empties and yet a nagging feeling persists, too little time, too much to do. Unrealistic expectations, the antagonist while the mind the protagonist both commiserate, and life becomes less about love, more about the need—the need to know, the need to define, the need for time.

Children know what they want. Usually it is candy or a toy. Regardless, they quickly verbalize their request, and when they don't get it, they move on to someone else hoping for the answer they want—"yes". As adults, we want to know, we *need* to know, answers, proven hypotheses, and defined unknowns are the driving forces of adulthood. Peace of mind, comically, germinates from erroneous clarifications muddled by scientists in an attempt to prove that which perplexes the mind. Fallaciously, the mind settles for "proof" discovered, and all is right with the world. We know two plus two equals four, we know the sky is blue, we know that if we throw a ball against a wall, it will return at the same angle at which it was thrown—this is what our minds "know," but our knowledge runs much deeper. Sure we can write a mathematical proof and intellectually discern 2 + 2, if someone were to say that the sky is purple, we would criticize and mock them, and sure, we could experiment with a ball and prove that it will come back. But what do we really know? What if early mathematicians and philosophers proved that two plus two equals five? What if blue as we know it today were labeled purple and purple labeled blue? We would believe it and blindly follow what we have been told for the mind is at ease with its "knowledge" even when there is no concrete, tangible evidence... Ah, but the mind is at ease, or is it?

The sun begins to settle into the night sky, and the day is coming to a close. One hectic day complete. How many more to come? The brilliance of the sky warms the heart and a flash of thought, a familiar feeling overtakes the soul. Is it... Could it be love? The onset of the day, a promise of the heart, love, peace, and joy but a brief glimpse in the waking dawn. Nothing is impossible for life invigorated in love makes life effortless. We can fight, we can claw our way through life, or we can move with ease for we know every step taken, every tear shed, every laugh uttered is purposed with God. Life is not a solo ride but rather a tandem ride. Sometimes, we take the lead, and other times, we take the backseat to God. A cluttered, anxious mind races, the body unsettled, and it tosses and sleep but a dream.

Why can we awaken in love and yet retire in worry? What do we know? Why do we feel the need to glorify the discoveries of knowledge

as determined by others and negate the intimate knowledge of the heart? Knowledge of the heart, the pinnacle truth, cannot be calibrated by the mind for the mind taints the truth, not to deliberately deceive but to delineate fact from fiction. Differentiating fact from fiction totes a fine line for the discerned fiction of the mind is the factual matter of the heart. Hence, we can arise for the day filled with love and turn in for the night riddled with worry and pain. Synthesis, the key to the human dilemma of the heart versus the mind, is achieved through trust,; trust in the promise of love intimately whispered with each cool breeze and the dawning of each new day. We feel it, we breathe, we hear it, we know it, and now we need to live it, live the love of the heart. Truth of the heart, love in the soul—this is the reality the mind seeks yet never sees. Skewed by the flaws of humanity, we must turn to the heart for here truth lies, here God lies whispering simple truths, promises of love. Philosophers and mathematicians will continue to make new discoveries, but the most important discovery—the most life-giving discovery, and yes, maybe the most controversial discovery—is the discovery of the heart, the dwelling place of God. What do we know? We know God, and we know love. Listen closely as the "wordless words" of the soul again speak. Listen for discovery will bring peace, love, and joy throughout the chaos and anxiety of our flawed humanity as these words heal our wounds and reconnect our heart with God:

Prayer
Connecting with God
How do I long for his innocent truth
How do I seek his majestic benevolence

Prayer
Rational blinders
I hear a gentle call amongst the angry winds
I see compassion amidst a broken heart

Prayer
Overwhelming love
Talents manifested in hope
Freedoms ventured in faith

Prayer
Emotional overload
Foreign feelings subject to ridicule
Logic disproved

Prayer
Our soul exposed
God alive in our actions
God pronounced in our wisdom

Prayer
Adventure to the heart
Journey to the soul
Beauty that lies within
God connection obvious

Prayer
God surrounds
God abound

God within
God infinite

Prayer
God with us

God's answer: unconditional love, truth, understanding, and companionship. God is with us, every second of the day, every moment of the night. Our struggles are no longer fretful, no longer intimidating for God embodies the soul. The joy, the bliss, the love was found within, for the soul is the very dwelling place of God. Looking past the human encumbrances of fear, peer pressure, deadlines, and self-criticism, a novel, unfamiliar and surreal feeling overtakes the mind. Surrendering to these feelings, we gaze into the mirror only to find God staring back. Fearful, we sheepishly look away, hiding from our very selves. Mustering the courage to look back into the mirror, the face of God still recognized as our own. Fixated upon this image, a deluge of affirming feelings validate the solace of God within us.

Having spent years surviving, by creating an iconic, prevaricated societal clone bolstered by worthless, distaining ideals resulted in the loss of self, the loss of unconditional self-acceptance, the demise of our godly worthiness. Striking with love and valor, God again presented his love with open arms and an invitation to partake in a faith journey, unfettered by strife, liberated by love. Anxious and with trepidation flooding the heart, the mirror haunts and dauntingly calls as if to prove that the reflective image is but a shadow of the experience. Timidly, we venture to the mirror, wanting, longing, hoping, and we find the same reflection as before, a loving invitation of God's presence, God's love

dwelling within our physical being. Our newfound purpose in life is that of unconditional acceptance, unconditional love, and unconditional self-judgment. Trust is the cornerstone of this epiphany, for to trust God with our whole heart is to sequester the mind from that which constricts and inhibits its survival, conjured reality. Cognizant of such a dichotic reality, we long for joy, peace, and love knowing the truth, God's wisdom dwells among our person, fueling our very soul. Freedom paves the way of the soul, our steps jovial, for our life is now burgeoning with love, protected by God. As the days pass, strength is gained, for we are unencumbered by that which society deems vital, prudent, or important. Setting aside egotistical, logical thought arouses a sense of worthiness, of altruism and a sense of belonging. Our invitation to God to take the reigns of our life results in unconditional love, judgment free lives where we have the freedom to be ourselves: to feel, free to laugh, free to cry, free to hurt, free to question without ridicule. It is in this freedom that we are awakened in love, comforted in peace, and rejuvenated in joy.

As I previously mentioned, I underwent the challenge of silencing the mind to journey to the soul via the mirror. An intensive exercise with a likewise intensive result: I found love, discovered joy and dependent trust. The happiness I sought, the many reinventions of my person brings not tears, but laughter to my soul. I did not need to travel to find the discovery of a lifetime, the discovery of life, my life. I carried joy, though I desperately sought happiness. The complexities of the human mind placate, they keep us wanting, searching for that which already lies within us ...joy.

This joy can carry us. It can lead to such spiritual awakenings where the warmth of the soul protects even in the coldest of climates. These climates, be they physical or spiritual, speak profound wisdom, encouraging the heart to lead the mind. When our unconscious speaks, we listen for we are truly silent and hear the wordless words of the heart. It was a dream which spoke, a dream which called, a dream which invited God, here, the dream of the heart, the dream for the heart. Let me share it with you....

> Walking through the forest, I noticed there among the trees an owl hides. Perched in the tree, he listens to hear the crack of a branch or the snap of a twig that will signal his prey. I stop and study the owl, though his feathers almost disappear into the bark. His patience is astounding; his sense of hearing, magnanimous. He sits and waits. It is in the stillness that I hear a babbling brook. Curious, I search for this water source. The first path leads to a dark, desolate cave—one which I dare not enter in the still cold. I begin to sweat. Fear paralyzes me. The thought of the unknown coupled with the dank darkness sends chills up my spine as if an evil presence were in my midst.

I turn to walk away. Something tells me to run. In my haste, I have forgotten my way. I reach out to pull back the shrubs and feel a deep prick. Blood pours forth. Clearly, what I thought to be shrubs were overgrown rose bushes complete with piercing thorns.

Quickly, I survey my surroundings and recall my search for the babbling brook. My efforts, my pain will not be in vain! I turn my focus to finding the brook, yet my attention is self-centered, and my chosen path filled with thistles. Deep into the path, I step over a boulder only to hear that unmistakable rattle. Knowing I have startled a rattlesnake, I am motionless and become as still as stone. Surveying my surroundings, I notice a large rock at my foot. With stealth and poise, I slowly pick up the large rock and smash the snake. Fearful of more hideous and treacherous encounters, I dare not go further along this path.

I turn and retrace my steps to my starting point. I look around and find the sign marked "Rattler Trail." The world around me becomes insignificant as I am too absorbed in my own agenda; it is as though I am viewing my world through a pinhole. I attempt to look and listen to

my surroundings, but the glistening sun upon the tree distracts me; the treetops look as though they are on fire. I turn towards the trees and quickly find myself upon them. In an instant, the sun sets, and the only thing that remains is darkness. I maneuvered through the woods although I lost focus, and I was not sure in which direction to walk. I become frightened, and the sounds of the forest at night are unfamiliar. I shiver with fear as my body feels the temperature drop. Unable to see the hand in front of my face, I sit and cower for it is fear that

Meredith Freed

55

keeps me here. After what seems like an eternity, my nerves settle, and I realize that it was my lack of attention to my surroundings that determined my position. So I simply stop and listen. I hear the owl. I see the branches move with the slight breeze of the wind. The forest is still but it no longer frightens. Tired from my long journey, I rest under a tree. The rising of the sun warms my body, and I awaken. Finally, attentive to my surroundings, I regroup and again begin my quest for the babbling brook. The forest looks different, greener, more inviting. I choose my path wisely, for I have learned the patience of the owl.

This path, filled with flowering trees and woodland creatures, calls to me. With each step, I take in the beauty of nature. I look as if through the eyes of God. I feel the presence of God. God is in my midst. The path is long but worth the energy spent listening and looking, enjoying the path instead of using it only for a destination. I see the brook ahead and begin to run, quickly forgetting the valuable lesson learned earlier. My hands dive into the brook. The sting of the cold incites anger, and I quickly remove my hand as if the brook were a live being that bites. I pout as a three-year-old child and haphazardly wander, following the path naturally carved by the babbling of the brook. Eventually, I come to a lake. I run to the waters edge and peer over. I cannot get a clear look at my reflection for something is troubling the water, so I move to another section of the lake. I got the same result. I just want to see, yet the water is so troubled at times that I barely see the reflection of the trees. Completely aggravated, I sit. From a distance, the water is not troubled, and a beautiful reflection of the forest is created. Again, I rush to the water's edge. Ripples, no reflection. I scream. A gentle wind caresses my cheeks, and with it, I hear, "If you do what you always did, you will get the same result."

Thinking clearly, I slowly approach the water. The ripples are not as obtrusive, and I begin to see my reflection. Upon further study of my reflection, I realize it was me all along. I was troubling the water, for in my rush to see, I was blinded to my own foot in the water causing a wake. I sit at the edge of the water. Silence overtakes me, patience overtakes me, and I become aware of the beauty of the lake. My eyes are opened to the wonder of the day, my heart open to God. As I sit in the stillness, I realize that I am not alone, that the anxiety and anger I had felt days, hours, moments earlier dissipated, leaving only peace.

This journey of the heart to settle the mind began with a walk through the thicket of the forest. I fully understand this fear. What is behind the brush? How will I be prepared? What if I do not find the right words? I cannot become vulnerable so this thicket serves as my protection. These thoughts and many more have rushed through my mind. The fear of exposing a less than perfect self was enough to keep me building my fortress, stone by stone that my heart may be protected. The funny thing was that no matter how high I erected the fortress, no matter how thick the walls, the melody of my heart still played, God still spoke to me, He still called me home. Finally, I trusted, I believe my foundation to be built on solid rock, grounded in Christ's love and so I listen, listen to the melody of my soul.

The melody of the heart still plays. It still invites, for the intrigue and suspense gravitate the soul to higher levels, God levels. But the meditative prayer, the longings, the overwhelming wordless words are saved for the lake, for it was this particular spot which brought about an epiphany—God in person, God in each one of us. Visions seen not simply with the eyes, true vision requires sight with the heart. Slow down, settle, stop—these are words which society looks upon with disdain for they infringe upon "knowledge" and attainment of goals. Ironically, it is the stopping at nothing and the curiosity-driven mind which often causes us to lose sight of our goals. The vision of the lake, the rattlesnake trail, the dark, cold fear—these can be catalysts for change so desperately needed as beauty is discovered, not just in the physical but in the spiritual dwellings lying in the depths of the heart. Stop and listen to the "wordless words" of God, and life will be forever altered. The mind will slow, the heart will lead, and the path through the forest will become an easily maneuvered path, overgrown brush and all. Allowing peace to take its forthright place in the heart, we refocus our purpose. Our goal of joy is attainable, for the love of God is felt. It is understood, and it is relied and acted upon that we may live, free of conditions and saturated in love. When sight is lost, we must remember to slow down, settle down, stop, and listen to the "wordless words" eloquently spoken from the heart for it instinctively knows the way, the path, of and to God.

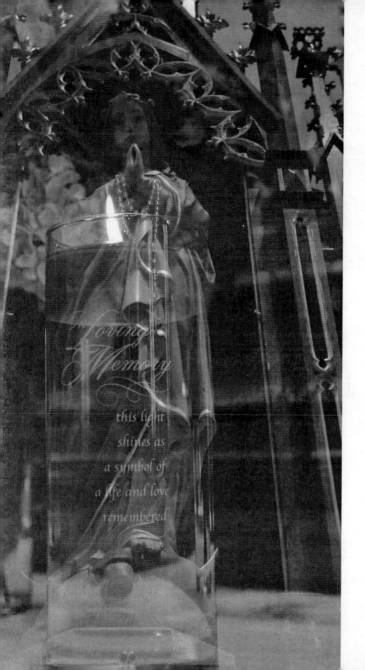

Loving Memory

this light
shines as
a symbol of
a life and love
remembered

Visions of Wisdom

Visions of Wisdom

Recognizing our vision, seeing our worth, allowing our heart to blossom in the unconditional love of God can be a daunting task for the words of the heart often contradict the words of society. Our challenge is to see the beauty that God sees, and hear the gentle words of God for He constantly speaks of unconditional love. Prayer is our avenue of connection with the reality of God.

How do we pray? Do we listen? The heart speaks and we know, we know the truth of these words yet we are taught to ignore them for the only credible words in the human language are those backed by research and proven by theorems. God whispers His wordless words and yet we hear for we need not ears to hear. We need to learn to listen, a lesson I learned and only completely understood at the death of my mother. For in my complete surrender to the love of God I came to understand love. I came to be love that I may share this love with others. I now know the heart. God's dwelling is His purposeful way of showing love that He may connect with us, that He may become one with His creation...us.

Looking back, I look with love, not sadness of the last days of my mother's death, for I know the truth of God's presence, the peace that He gave to her was a peace that is undiscoverable here on this earth. Her spirit rested as her breathing slowed yet she feared not for she was enveloped in the love of God. Often I think back to her death, saddened of course, but thankful for this expression of trust she offered. Now, when I look into the mirror I see love and when I look into the eyes of my child, I feel love for I know and understand God's presence amongst us. As my daughter and I embrace, I am reminded to slow down, to enjoy that which surrounds us, that which has been put forth for us. In every flower, God's beauty is present; in each gust of wind, God's omnipotence is felt; in each new sunrise, the love of God warms saddened hearts.

God has taught me how to embrace life. No longer do I burden my days with must do's for they only hold me back from the want to's of the heart. I have become a flower vastly soaking in the glory of the Son, willing to learn, willing to put aside the chatter of the mind and follow the lessons of the heart, the lessons of love intimately offered by a loving Creator. Stop and listen to the words of the heart. They speak for you, they speak to you, of love, of acceptance, of greatness, of God.

It is not enough to say that we believe in God and what he has revealed to us. We need to feel God, give to God all that we are, all that we have, all that we require. God hears our cries. He answers our prayers, yet we do not see, for we are blinded as we look with our eyes and do not seek with our heart. Should we let the heart lead, we will no longer be encumbered by fear, by disbelief, by devastation, for the presence of God is mightier than superficial sight.

"Look with your eyes and not with your hands" was a constant reminder from our youth. What if we looked with our heart and not with our eyes? We would find God, humbly dwelling within us. How has

God been felt today? As logical beings, we are petrified of feelings for we believe feelings to be deceptive and cause pain; we become suspicious and ignore feelings with the erroneous notion that they portray weakness. I thought myself unworthy of God's love though I believed it true for others. I knew God loved me but I felt I had not yet proven myself to Him. Little did I know that the proof was only for me, vainglory, a show of ignorance tactfully hidden in the pursuit of independence. The more I fought to become who I wanted to be, the more I became lost, the harder I prayed but forgot to listen. It was not until I truly gave into the heart and learned to feel did I embrace this offering of love. Deeply engaged in our emotion, we are at our strongest, for it is here that God protects, guides, and loves us for all that we are. Flaws included. It is in the loss of sight that we begin to see, for we feel the presence of God among us, within us, within others. It is in the loss of our hearing that the wordless words are heard as if spoken with a megaphone of the soul. The powerful presence of God permeates our being, permitting us to experience our soul. A soul experience is nothing short of faith wrapped in feelings. Feelings alive, vibrant in color, doused with the scent of honeysuckle, we are granted the freedom to sense God in the beauty and complexity of faith. No longer are we staunch or stoic, for we now understand faith. It has been passionately felt, convincingly spoken, and vividly seen in the reflection of the soul—a soul seen in the beauty of faith, a soul experienced in the depths of prayer. I must admit that my prayer life has drastically changed since listening to my heart. Conversations are daily and meditations of love counteract the anxiety of the day all because I took a chance and trusted.

How do we hear God? Would we recognize God if we were in a crowd of people or do we "save" God for church? God is all around us, in all that we do, in every person with whom we interact, in every consoling touch received and offered. God *is*. When we stop to actually contemplate this notion, we become overwhelmed. God in everything? Wow, that means we can't get away from God, that everything we do, good and bad, is seen by God. While this idea is supposed to comfort, it often overwhelms. Newton proved that for every action, there is an equal and opposite reaction. As humans, we apply this principle to all aspects of life, even God, whether consciously or unconsciously.

Our thoughts migrate, "If God is always around, sees all, and knows all, then we don't need to pray because he already knows." Okay, so you like to ride the roller coaster. You have ridden it a million times. If you are given the opportunity to ride it again, do you take it? Of course you do! You know the feeling of excitement that comes across you as you twist and turn at high speeds with your hands flying high in the air and the shrills come from the mouth of babes. Knowing the feelings the roller coaster would incite did not stop you from getting a ticket. Rather, it was the very push you needed to buy the ticket. The same is true with God. This notion that God *is* can be our calming

grace and ease our mind as we come to understand that we do not walk alone. The first ride of the roller coaster more than likely caused trepidation, anxiety, and maybe a little queasiness, but when the ride came to a screeching halt, feelings of excitement and accomplishment trumped the fears and sparked interest in another ride. Our initial introduction to God, this idea that God *is*, is so unfathomable. How can God be omnipresent and omnipotent? As we settle our mind and begin to feel God, we lead with our heart *because* God knows. Leading with our heart in our society can leave us beaten, bloody, and broken. But leading with our heart to God can be the healing touch we so desperately desire.

"God, I don't know what to say. I don't know what I am doing, where I am going. Help." This is a fine prayer. Somewhere along the line, we come to understand that all our prayers must be perfectly composed, perfectly prayerful. But God *is*. Our prayers are not for God but to God. In our conversations with God, we come to know God more fully as we would come to know a friend, but we also come to know our very selves more fully. As in any relationship, there are times of elation, of sorrow, of confusion, of pain, of anger all feelings, which God understands. Keeping these feelings from God only makes us callous and even resentful. God does not judge us. He does not laugh nor does he mock us. He loves us unconditionally. He has equipped us with many talents, virtues, and relationships which allow us to experience this love. Thus the "wordless words" are again spoken but this time acknowledged by the mind as well as the heart. This is what I often hear when I go to write or silence myself in meditation. The wordless words speak to me and now I listen...

"Do you remember when you first called my name, frantically searching for me, and you found me right by your side the entire time?

Do you remember the first time you were hurt, and I caught each tear that fell from your swollen eyes?

Do you remember when, in silence of the night, darkness crept into your heart, almost paralyzing you, yet day came and you recovered?

Do you remember I told you not to be afraid, but you were, yet everything turned out fine?

Do you remember the kind stranger who offered you a free lunch the very day you forgot your money?

Do you remember when your dad offered you the coat of his back when you were cold?

Do you remember when someone you thought was a friend had betrayed your trust, the whole world seemed lost, yet love and friendship found you once again?

Do you remember when you stood back and let others take credit for your amazing work? Well, I noticed

Do you remember using your gift of diplomacy to temper heated discussions?

Do you remember seeing the world through the eyes of a child, where everything was yours for the taking and nothing was tainted?

Do you remember the trepidation you felt when the word *unconditional* was used in the context of trust, love, and joy?

Do you remember the song that played in your heart the first time you felt unconditional love?

Do you remember the many times you were disliked, mocked, jeered at for doing what was right?

Do you remember the first time you prayed with a friend and how your heart leapt with joyful amazement with the feeling of completion this gave?

Do you remember the anxieties created when trying to do everything yourself and how the load lightened significantly when you let me help?

Do you remember when loneliness was all you knew, and then you found me?

Do you remember when some random stranger smiled at you and made your day?

Do you remember when you opened the Bible, and the verses spoke to your very soul?

Do you remember crying with a friend, feeling her pain, and wanting to take it away?

Do you remember the look on the young kid's face that got a Christmas present for the first time in ten years?

Do you remember the pain on the widow's face as you took her hand and said, "I am listening"?

Do you remember cuddling in on the couch, in the arms of a loved one, knowing that security was yours?

Do you remember crying yourself to sleep thinking all hope was lost, yet faith found you again?

Do you remember my promise of unconditional everything?

Remember all these times, the good and painful. Each brings with them a lesson, a lesson of love that can be shared with others. Cherish these for they are reminders that I will always be with you. You see what others refuse to see, you comprehend what others do not understand, you hear what others ignore, and you feel what others rationalize away. Now go, help others feel, and know what you know. Help them to create memories of their own that will bring them a lifetime of joy!

Love,

God

It is in the discerning of our gifts, listening to our heart, experiencing God within the beauty of our very soul that we are permitted to accept God's unconditional love for us. Acceptance of such love comes first from our acceptance and love of self, something which cannot be brought to light without our intrinsic and intimate knowledge of God experienced exclusively through prayer.

Prayer is the most powerful tool we carry along on our journey. This tool, when used properly, creates grandiose landscapes, breathtaking portraits, and incredible abstractions. Though God always answers our prayers, we sometimes misunderstand what it is exactly we are asking. When we pray for patience, the gift does not come wrapped with a bow, card attached saying, "Here's the patience you requested."

Instead, we are given opportunities to practice our prayer request of patience. Each circumstance presents an opportunity for growth. This notion holds true for self-discovery. Upon discernment of God within self, we begin to see a glimpse of our true character, of the qualities and talents which set us apart, that make us unique. I feared this discernment for I feared not the discovery of talents but the intrinsic desire to boast about these talents, to elevate one to a high status for selfish gains. This is one point with which I still struggle for I believe humility to be our grounding, the foundation by which all love grows, all life is absorbed into the grace of God. Integrating these gifts into our lives is often a difficult task. With each implementation, we gain a sneak peek of courage and trust believed to be independent of our being yet ever ingrained in our personhood. We convince ourselves that such gifts only come out when needed, when the situation calls for courage or trust. What we fail to understand is that we are courage, we are trust, and we are the love of God within. Our prayer for self-discovery brings with it, not only a flash of who we are but various opportunities to examine and develop our character. The courage uncovered in the purest of hearts is not simply tested in awkward or difficult situations. Rather, it shines that it may become what it was intended to be—us. Our "God connection" is never broken, even when ignored, tossed aside, or forgotten, for our prayers always lie within the depths of our soul, they are the palpitations of the heart.

What is our driving force: humility, grace, patience, ego, pride, or intolerance? Pursuing God is our heart's call of freedom, to freedom, for our God connection frees with dependence. Where do we search? How do we listen? The answers are revealed in the stories told by believers so long ago. Strength is the silence spoken in the wordless words of God. What exactly is strength? David had strength to defeat Goliath, Elijah had strength to hear God's call and answer, and Peter had the strength to endure a horrific death. Unfortunately, there is a dichotomy between biblical and societal strength. Today, strength is a physical measurement. How far one is willing to manipulate others for purely selfish reasons? What lengths will be taken to ensure victory, receive honors, or remain on top? Or how much weight one can physically hold without assistance? It is about the individual, autonomous pride gaining power. This

Stand tall

superficial strength is a self-inflated ego boost, which is quickly deflated by failure and misfortune. True strength, God's strength, is humility. True strength is epitomized in the innocence of the baby Jesus. A child wrapped in swaddling clothes and lying in a manger, exposed to the cold, reliant not only on his parents but the kindness of strangers. This is our king. It is not until we put aside our agenda, our wants, our misconstrued understanding of reality and allow God to take control do that we become strong.

Strength is merely a manipulation of the childhood game of hide-and-seek. It is not until we surrender our fabricated realities that true strength

Live boldly

is gained. Doors begin to open, new paths carved through the chiseled stone, for we are empowered to take on challenges that would otherwise leave us paralyzed. We do all of this, not alone but enveloped in God's love and tenderness. By all rights, the Philistine should have easily overpowered David, a young shepherd. But David's invitation to God made the difference between life and death for the people of Israel. Elijah could have easily ignored God's call and continued to follow his own dreams but instead be heard God in the gentlest breeze and said yes to a life of ridicule but beauty. Peter, filled with fear, denied Jesus, his best friend, to save his own life, but humbled by this experience, he turned to God for forgiveness, and as his pride subsided, he was martyred for his faith. These men exhibit true strength, God strength. For it is in setting aside worldly ties, societal norms and prideful constrictions that we find strength within our very soul.

I am not labeling myself as great among the stories of God, please do not think this. I have felt God call to me. Looking back at my past, I can honestly say that God has fervently called my name though I often did not hear. Over the years, I attended retreats and coordinated retreats and one technique often practiced is a timeline of life events. In performing this exercise myself, I began to see patterns in my life that I never noticed while immersed in minutia of life. There, in black and white, God spoke. You must understand that I was a perfectionist. I would not stop until things were perfect. Thus delegation was often a difficult task for me. I ran through life with the must do that and have to do this. Life quickly became a feverish game of catch up accompanied by sleepless nights at the end of which I would wind up run down to the point of exhaustion and sickness and then, only then, would I stop.

While attending a busy person's retreat, my spiritual director confronted me with this pattern and said, "Don't you think God is trying to tell you something?" I was floored. My sickness could be God's speech? Later that night I reflected on the words of Sister Kathy as tears streamed down my cheeks for she was exactly right. God was speaking to me and I hadn't heard a word He was saying. I now carry the words of Sister Kathy with me for when life becomes so encumbered by that which is unnecessary, I remember to listen to God, listen to His wordless words. Sickness still plagues me as it does all humans, but not in the fashion it did for I have learned the truth of strength, the truth of our journey. Strength is not about what we can hold. It is about who is holding us. Can we humble ourselves that we may be held by God, that we may find joy and beauty in all that is around us even in the midst of turmoil? Strength, no longer a measurement, rather an experience in humility, is our connection of faith.

Believing Is Seeing—The Eyes of the Heart

Believing Is Seeing—The Eyes of the Heart

Graciously, we bow to an omnipresent God who unconditionally accepts, supports, and listens to our every plea, our every whimper, and answers with such a deep love that life itself becomes more overwhelming. And so we live, we breathe, we feel alive for God has imparted his wisdom, his peace, himself wrapped in the guise of faith.

Faith can take us to new heights, allow us to see new places, even be the tour guide on exciting adventures. Yet faith can only begin to root when the heart feels, the heart accepts, the heart embraces God's gift of unconditional love. Unconditional, such a foreign word in our society, yet it is ours for the taking if only we acknowledge our heart, the dwelling place of God. When life hands us lemons, we are to make lemonade. The amazing thing about faith is that when life hands us lemons, we are able to make orange juice, for anything is possible with God. Our faith, our most treasured possession, does not need to be hidden in a box for safekeeping to ensure it will not be stolen. The beauty of this gift is that it grows exponentially when used. It can be contagious, and most importantly, no one can take it from us. Faith is our gift to cultivate, to use, to lean on, to depend upon, to allow us to see the pure heart, the image of self, fully vested in God. Societal pressures, materialism, status quo, obligations—these all attempt to block our relationship with God for they deal purely with the rational, the logical and leave no room for intuitive knowledge of God. Faith, our God connect, our gentle reminder that we are not alone in this world, can take us on grandiose adventures. Life, propelled by faith, becomes a dichotomy of placid joy. The peace settles our soul while the joy ignites and inspires commitment and introspection into the life of God—our very own life. Implicit trust and constant honesty keep us searching for God in new and exciting realms of our existence. As our search for God widens, our roots deepen that our base may support rapid growth in the truth and love of God. As our faith matures, our roots spread and gain strength in the love, support, and protection of those with whom we affiliate. Though it may seem outrageous to find peace in death, I can honestly say walking with a dear friend as he journeyed in faith in the last months of his earthly life helped to complete the circuit of faith. Knowing the end of the physical life does not mean the end of our life came to fruition as I walked with my friend and experienced what he experienced in his last waking hours. He knew, without a doubt, the love of God. He would recount what he saw, what he felt as he silenced his mind and let God carry him. As we prayed, God settled the anxiety of the situation that we could hear His words. And as he took his last breath I knew he truly found peace for his faith was rooted in love, reconnected to our Heavenly Father. In this life, we are given the opportunity to become one with others, to walk, to journey, to experience the life breath of God as we become connected with one another via the heart.

Roots of one tree intertwined, knotted, entangled among the roots of a nearby tree permit both to grow ever taller. Years pass and both trees stand tall providing shade and beauty to a well-manicured landscape. The roots become the topic of conversation. Everyone seems to have an opinion, a comment, about the entangling of these roots and how it will eventually inhibit growth and cause both trees to die. But the gardener pays no attention, for he understands the uniqueness of his garden and continues to cultivate that which has been planted. One may be an oak, and the other, a chestnut, but the success of both trees is dependent upon, not independent of, the other. These roots have intrinsically grown in a braid-like pattern that no matter the storm, no matter how violent the winds these trees will stand tall and grow ever taller. This support structure, unique as it is, is grounded in deep, elongated, entangled roots now reaching down to the earth below, which provides the necessary nutrients for the trees to blossom, to maximize each tree's potential, to become a mighty oak and a grandiose chestnut. Years continue to pass, the trees continue to grow and produce with the roots entangled, growing ever stronger, ever taller. The landscape is beautiful and breathtaking, all because the mighty oak and grandiose chestnut learned to lean, learned to trust, learned that flowering buds come from faith—shared faith. In sharing a gift, the gift is used, possibly to its fullest potential. Faith explored, faith endured becomes faith alive, for we begin to see life through the eyes of God—no blinder, no tint, and life as it was intended, fully loving, fully unconditional, fully saturated in hope, stimulating the heart to silence the mind. God's wisdom expanded the heart to accept faith, the intimate gift tenderly bestowed upon us yet fully our responsibility to open and use.

Faith, a private conviction of a truth revealed to an individual in a unique and highly personal manner, is something most people hold close, for the thought of sharing faith with others paralyzes their very being. It is in this paralysis that we become withdrawn for fear of exposure to the elements of sarcasm, ridicule, and patronization.

Thoughts arise such as, "What if my faith is different?" "What if it is wrong?" and "What if I look like a fool?" I spent years hiding my faith though attempting to follow it; an oxymoron I know yet that was my life as I attempted to walk to the beat of society and live the humility of Christ. Life was difficult as I had to constantly remember which mask was worn in which situation. Being an only child, I wanted to fit in with others, never stick out and so I learned to silence my heart. Taught that God only gives us what we can handle, I began to contemplate this idea. I thought, "Wow, I must be a strong person for much has been thrown at me." But then I got to thinking it is not that God gives us anything bad. Situations happen, death occurs, life is what we make of it and yet God does not create this sadness. God, too, is saddened by our sadness; He cries at our tears; He laughs at our joys; we are connected. God is always there for us, loving, carrying, guiding us that we may become the very best person encompassed in love. Faith, my faith, was a gift from God that I may know, that I may become His offering of love. Embodying this faith permitted me to understand my heart and the richness of my soul, for I no longer worry about what others think of me. Faith is my breath. Faith is my source of life.

Faith, an intrinsically special gift from God, is developed in the midst of our distinctive talents leaving each of us an extraordinary opportunity to connect with God when and where we are most comfortable. We meet God when we are open to his revelation, for it is in the discovery of such magnanimous revelations that our gift of faith becomes our own. Faith, uncovered, discovered in the light of our person, in the light of our talents, is seeing God as we see ourselves. And thus, faith stares back, for nestled within our heart is our strongest desire to know, to relate, to identify, to define.

How are we defined? By who are we defined, who we long to become, or by what others project upon our person? We are taught that life is defined for us by our clothes, our speech, our life choices. Life is defined by one thing, one thing only—faith. Bombarded with sayings such as "go big or go home" or "just do it" demonstrates the falsehood that the illusion of control is not an illusion, but rather a reality which we must procure for life to be happy. This lifelong search for the American dream leaves with it feelings of disappointment, of shame, of failure, for all of the searching has left us weak, confused, and lonely. We continue life with a defeatist, somewhat skeptical attitude which taints future life decisions because we never completely grasped happiness. Having "gone big," we went home sad and unsuccessful. Happiness is a shallow mirage fictitiously dangled before us in an effort to keep semblance of order within the urban jungle. The problem with this mirage is just that—it is a mirage. Hopes and dreams are often replaced with resentment upon the discovery of this mirage. Time lost will not be time gained, thus creating a void. Sullen, calloused by life events, the challenge of life becomes greater, for it is now a desolate black hole, which extracts joy, but not necessarily happiness. Happiness, the superficial elixir of the control gods found only on the surface, quickly dissipates among the heartache and disappointment of a fundamental belief shared by most—that we control life. Those who comprehend and fully grasp that faith alone defines a person seemingly have found the secret to success in life. Defined by faith, we walk with God every second of the day; and when we tire, we are carried, for God's love penetrates the heart and the cold urban jungle becomes less frightening. Happiness, the lure of the mind, is no longer the driving force propelling life's "just do it" slogans. Trust, hope, and understanding become the critical tools in the arsenal of faith for happiness is no longer sought but rather the search is for joy. Following God, listening to God, hearing God without words, without noise, is faith for we know God and the soul speaks. Joy is found even in the lowliest of times for God dwells among us, within us, and life is whole. Allowing faith to define our lives, we become free, and we become love. Actions reflect our choices which reflect our heart—God. Life is no longer unsuccessful, for each step is carefully calculated by faith, gently enveloped in love, and critically centered in God. From the harsh lessons of the urban jungle to the contemplative realizations of the meditative prayers, God speaks, life is defined in terms of God, in terms of our willingness to listen and act in light of faith.

As a child, playtime was often spent spinning around, spying rainbows, chasing shadows, dancing in the rain—a life innocent and pure. There is something to be said about imagining a world of dragons and coloring the day away; a time when the biggest worry was if we could have mac and cheese for dinner followed by a huge bowl of ice cream. Life now involves the "have tos", the "must do now", and the most popular, "I don't have the time". We rush around slaves to deadlines and worry; instead of spinning to create fun, our head spins as a sign that we are out of control, and yet we continue this "adult" path. Eventually, we stop or at least pause, only to find a shell of an existence. Manipulated by societal pressure to conform, this urban jungle has set forth a narrow path, inlaid with logic, reason and science. If a theory cannot be rationally explained, then the theory is proven false and discarded. This routine has no room for the unknown, the felt, the God factor. For dealings with the heart are deemed as childish, as immature and weak. It's amazing. The very notion of strength, while along this path, is believed to come from the mind, to be emotionless; thus, we become a carbon copy of others with walls of protection surrounding the heart to guard against criticism and emotions. The very notion of not feeling, of not living the life God intended, of hiding or suppressing the characteristics which set us apart makes the path of life frightening and creates the need for the defensive wall. If we accept ourselves for who we are, love ourselves for where we are, follow our heart for what lies inside, develop our faith through prayer and introspection, seek the strength within our heart for how it can safeguard our worth and simply ask the question why without fear of embarrassment, life would regain its thunder, its appeal. Rainbows and rain dances would replace disgruntled meetings and deadlines, laughter would replace criticism, shadow-chasing would replace lurking in the shadows to hide from life. Life would not be spinning out of control. Life would be spinning with joy for laughter, love, and adventures are the byproducts of a faith-filled life. Faith, a developed relationship with God, deemed laughable on the playground, is now our saving grace in the playground of life. Live, love, laugh as a child, a child of faith living in an urban jungle, pressured to run with the pack of rational wolves. Two choices, the rational or the heart, which do you choose?

Hindsight is 20-20, and life lessons seem so clear when revisited with goggles of faith. How many times have we heard the expression, "If I knew then what I know now"? But we do know, for God dwells within our person, we know him, we trust him, we are overwhelmed by his love, yet we often choose to disbelieve our heart and ignore the "wordless words" spoken by God. Stifled by rational projections of irrational theories, we begin to view the world as judicial declarations reckoned by arbitrary rules fabricated by societal objections. In essence, we decide life's fairness with regard to our happiness and happenstances. Life becomes unfair when we do not get our way, yet it is completely fair when reconciled happiness tempers sullen behaviors. With this in mind, a question haunts the mind, "Whoever said life was fair?" Life is not fair. The earlier we come to terms with this truth, the earlier we come to understand that joy is not dependent upon external, tangible factors, rather, internal attributes of faith.

This is not to say that following and living our faith will lead to perfect lives without sorrow or pain. The fairness of life is not in question, rather this: "How will we play the hand we are dealt?" There are times we want ice cream so bad only to find that someone has put the carton back empty. Or in this vast game of life, the promotion goes to the slacker in the next cubicle who puts forth no effort, is constantly late, and, quite honestly, who in his jeans and ripped T-shirt, has no concept of "dress casual." Yet there he is, making twice the salary with twice the number of personal days. Fairness has nothing to do with life. Once we start to use the word *fair*, resentment, bitterness, and negativity consume our existence, and life is problematic. Instead of being thankful for what we have, we dwell on what we don't have and compare it to the fantastic things others do have and seemingly flaunt in our faces.

Life is about what we do with what we have that makes the difference. We may not have the hottest car or the coolest pair of kicks, yet we have a means of transportation and warm feet. Life is about perspective. We can play a constant game of keeping up with the Joneses, or we can be thankful for the things we do possess. Once we let go of our ego and surrender to God, life takes on an entirely different meaning. Life is enjoyable, life is placid, and life is humbled. Awakened with gratitude, we see life no longer as a dichotomy between the "have to" and "need to." Life simply becomes a "want to" with a smile. Sure, nothing is perfect. There will be awkward times, there will be difficult struggles, and there will be sadness, yet it is what we do in each of these times that make the difference. When we put on our "God-goggles," our view is no longer distorted by jealousy, rational thought, or hatred—it is driven by love, inspired by faith, and rested in diligence. Only we have the power to change our perspective, only we have the power to invite God into our lives, only we have the power to look at the glass as half full, only we have the power to change our lives. God will honor us, God will walk with us no matter the perspective chosen, yet life is more rewarding, more fulfilled with a "God-goggle" perspective and attitude. Gratefulness follows our footsteps while grace and humility lead the way. Life is about what we do with what we have and the difference is made by our procurement of faith.

Tires spinning, dirt flying, gas pedal floored, engine revved, frustration building, stuck, tires still spinning. Awareness is the key to the knowledge of what stands between our goals and us when faith is our tow truck. Stop, look, and listen—sound advice if only we were trained in such endeavors. Stopping, even for a second, in this world of "have to," "must do," and "needed yesterday," we run the risk of getting run over. Trained only to see that which is right before us, we quickly miss all that surrounds us, all that encompasses our daily lives, for our eyes are open, but our hearts are closed. Listen. In the still of the night, we hear absolute silence, yet we long to hear the voice of God beckoning as he did in the Old Testament. Why doesn't God talk anymore? Why, it seems, has God become mute in a world devoid of moral recognition, a world built on a foundation of science and logic, a world so desperately in need of spiritual awakening? God isn't mute. He speaks every day. The blinders placed on a horse in an effort to keep him focused are similar to our blinders, yet ours were a welcomed means of blocking rational thought. God fuels our lives with unconditional love, acceptance, worthiness, and fortitude, yet we often run away because we are unaware. Stop, look, listen to what lies behind, what stands before, and who stands beside us. Are our hearts and minds open? Can we hear? Do we see? For the obstacles which lie before us pale in comparison to the might of God which has been eloquently offered time and again yet declined, for in our subjective blindness, sight is lost. Yet we are pulled. Our heart feels. Our "God connect" is real. Eyes become open, hearts begin to see, and ears hear what the heart knows—God's love, God's voice speaking in the gentlest of winds. Aware, we stop, look, listen, and live the "wordless words" gently spoken by God. Tires spinning, dirt flying, gas pedal floored, engine revved, frustration building, stuck, tires still spinning, it is just mud, a little rocking, a little more gas, and the road is ours, next stop gas.

There are times in our lives that we feel we are weak, that exposure to a world filled with hatred, hurt, and devastation becomes our kryptonite. It is as though we fall short of our goals. The destination once in sight no longer exists, and inferiority complexes take the lead through a narrow path of tattered existence. As tears stream, labored breathing prompts the stoppage of the journey, but something from within keeps us trudging along though the scenery is grim and unfamiliar. Exhaustion sets in, the mind wanders, and yet wonders why, how, what will the next step on the rocky, unpaved path uncover? The racing thoughts cease as a gentle wind wipes away the sweat and tears. The body stills, the heart placid, the surroundings are less hostile, and the soul begins to settle. Surely, this transformation is the product of faith for it has proven itself a worthy adversary of despair. Yet something is different, the feeling of confidence, of determination, of assurance, fills the soul and the destination, once again on the radar, is within reach. The journey continues. The path is still windy with blind spots, dangerous twists, unpleasant surroundings and broken concrete among the stones and dirt. Strengthened by faith, courage is no longer a fabricated emotion but the foundation of our existence. We are strength, we are love, we are courage—both in times of struggle and times of joy.

God bestows upon us these gifts so gently, so quietly, so skillfully that we may not even know that we possess such virtues. Worry, sadness, anguish; the realness of the pain of such emotions can leave us to feel feeble and impotent, the furthest thing from strong. Yet we look into the mirror. We see our worth. We believe we deserve only the best, and we continue our journey. This is true "God strength." This is our gift in good times and bad.

It is in the difficult times that our strength is hidden for it carries us—it protects us. We are the strength, but it may go unrecognized. Without this strength, this courage, we would have stopped along the path, never continued, the fight lost, despair the victor. This is not the case, for today, we walk along the path, coupled with faith in God and the hand of a friend. The journey is bumpy, but it is nothing we cannot handle. With destination in sight, each step becomes a reassurance of our strength, still faced with challenges, yet they become less intimidating as trust is built from within. Faith and courage are the foundation, the building blocks of strength—the silent force within.

This is what faith has to offer if only we accept and acknowledge the gift entrusted to us in love. Faith, a burgeoning of the soul, effortlessly accepted in the "wordless words" of the heart is spoken to entice, spoken to revive the deflated desires pounced upon by the daily dealings of the mind, placated by the fairness of life. Armored with faith, life is restored to the "God settings" of the soul.

Compass of the Soul

Compass of the Soul

When we are lost, we have at our disposal a multitude of options by which we can regain our longitudinal placement and proceed upon our course. I am the type of person who has a rough idea where I am going and proceeds with caution, ever mindful of the direction I wish to visit. That being said, there are plenty of times when I find myself lost yet my stubborn ego will not allow me to stop and ask for directions, so I aimlessly wander until I successfully find my destination. The compass of my soul was no different in that I shied away from explorations of the heart in an attempt to master my feeling via the mask of logic. I attempted to fit faith into a logical formula to be evaluated like trigonometry with a single solution. While I was on a journey, I neglected to enjoy the journey. With my sights only on the destination, I became lost for every rest stop looked like the next. When passengers did accompany me, talk was lighthearted, without a sense of purpose or understanding of self. Then, along my journey I met my challenge, someone who allowed me to be myself, to identify with the God within me and celebrate my person. Quickly the journey became more about the journey and less about the destination for my golden compass had been identified as the source of love living within my person, known by God yet accepted by me. It was with the acceptance from my best friend that caused the invitation of the heart, for the heart to trust in that which perpetuates the heart... love.

While our journey of faith is a personal journey, the walk along this path need not be in solitude. We easily can become calloused, tired and sore as the uphill climb becomes arduous, and we are forced to rest. Cold and weary, we become startled at the sound of snapping twigs in the distant brush. Upon investigation of the surroundings, we find a stranger on a different path already inhabited. An invitation to journey with this stranger is extended; however, with the face shadowed and the voice muffled by the howling wind, the offer is accepted with reluctance. We travel the path in silence as the beauty of the wooded path slowly unfolds with the brilliance of the rising sun. With each ray of light, the path becomes clearer, the hue of the leaves more vibrant, and the stranger more familiar. The trepidations subside and a blissful spirit overtakes this journey as the stranger is unmasked and recognized as a trusted friend endowed with the love of God. The journey, which began in solitude, now continues in the company of a confidant. To embark upon the path of faith with another is to uncover hidden trails within the forest. Trails thought to be too treacherous, too unstable become trails sought after, for we know that if we lose our footing, someone will be there to catch us. Paths overgrown with thickets and thorns are no longer deemed hazardous for the revelation of the darkness of our soul has not sent our sidekick running yet remaining ever close, experiencing every sound, every sight, every touch of God the path has to offer. Challenging trails only solidify this blossoming friendship, as trust becomes the cornerstone to a celebration of a faith journey. These wanderers know not what life holds or what the next trail will uncover, but they do know that whatever is revealed, good or bad, they have each other. As gold is tested in fire, so too friendship is tested in faith, for it is God who brings faith and a friend who reveals God.

Our revelation of God within comes from our acceptance of self. Since we cannot give what we do not have, we must first inventory the trophies of our heart. Jesus's command to love our neighbor as ourselves poignantly calls attention to our love of self. If we do not recognize love, how can we give love? We spend hours, even years, attempting to camouflage our very person that we may not be recognized as an outsider. Years of hiding and we become a stranger to ourself as our constant masquerading reflects an alien image startling the onlooker. I am no stranger to this attempt of camouflaging that which causes feeling so others may not see the truth of my heart for the truth was my heart yearned to know love. I spent most of my years doing for others and neglecting my personal needs. I saw this as fulfilling the Greatest Commandment, loving my neighbor without thought of anything in return. Again, at a retreat, I was challenged by this scripture passage as the leader asked me to define love. Thinking it an obvious question, I responded with self-sacrifice. Proudly I answered for I could not be wrong, thus my years spent doing for others. To my surprise, the leader smiled and said "no". I was baffled as she continued, "Love, my friend, while it may include self-sacrifice, is not limited by such stringent constraints. Love embodies our person. It makes us feel warm, safe and genuinely important through the eyes of another." She continued to speak about love and its importance in our lives as well as our spiritual connections. I was still stuck on the definition so I did not follow the rest of the lecture. I did, however, catch something to the fact that I couldn't give love if I didn't have love. I turned in for the night perplexed at the unraveling of the day. The next day the retreat concluded and we parted ways. I continued to pray this passage in hope that its truth would somehow hit me over the head; it did. I spent most of my life loving my neighbor and not even liking me. Why? I knew not the true meaning of love and furthermore did not believe myself worthy of said love for this love was reserved others but not me. Acceptance of truth, acceptance of self, is not an easy task in an egotistical, glory-sought society. Yet the task is at hand and the prize, life changing. Connecting with our spirit, kindling the love, the peace, the truth which dwells within the very depths of our soul, calls for a transformation of self. Offerings of love, faith, hope, truth, fortitude, knowledge, and understanding have been graciously bestowed upon us throughout our life. Gifts have been placed before us, and our job is to learn how to use each gift to its fullest potential.

Climbing a mountain is never easy. It is especially difficult when we are ill-equipped. But with the right tools, the treacherous climb becomes a minuscule hill. The same is true for our journey with God. With the right equipment, life is no longer a challenge, rather an adventure. True, adventures have twists and turns, peaks, and valleys, but they bring a sense of accomplishment, a sense of security, a sense of peace. At the day's end, we may have no idea which path was correct, which path led us in the wrong direction, but what we do know is that the trip was worth every bump, bruise, or battle wound we incurred. While these wounds heal, we look back in reflection of the day's events and find that we have become stronger, more courageous, and more loving. As we gently clean our equipment, we find the precious tools of faith, hope, love, temperance, and fortitude. Setting these tools aside, we find one that was so buried in the pile, it almost looked like rubble—the tool of friendship. As monumental as these virtues are, friends—people we can trust and be ourselves with, people we can lean on, who will hold us up, carry when needed—are the most significant and treasured of tools. True friendship is vital to the adventure for if this tool was not uncovered or if it were never placed in the bag, the adventure would have become a nightmare with hope for a rescue that never occurred. But this tool is in our bag, so the questions now are, "How do we use this tool? Where do we start this seemingly haphazard journey without an instruction manual or a map?"

TRUST—Timely Real Utterances of Single Truths. Trust, the most provocative of virtues, is also the most petrifying as it can stimulate or debilitate the soul within seconds. At the very depth of our soul lies trust. A soul's perspective thrives on trust. It depends on the "wordless words" intimately spoken by a confidant, one with whom our personhood is safe and never mocked. Yet there will be times when trust is tempered, it is tested for life events will prove judgmental and derogatory. Just as the sand is heated to extremely high temperatures to form glass, our trust in another is tempered with actions. The integrity with which these actions are performed speaks to our heart, discovering a canvas of the soul. Look into the mirror, and trust stares back. Who to trust, when to trust, and what to trust?

Upon further investigation of trust, we find that it is a reflection, a reflection of self—mirror of the soul, mirror of love, mirror of a pure spirit.

God speaks, a reflection of God, a reflection of love, a reflection of self. The grains of sand are the obstacles of the heart, under pressure and heat, the sand forms glass. Under the guise of love and trust, we become reflections of Godly love. Trust—the reason for friendship, the reason for peace, the reason for love—is at the core of our being. Taking shape, growing, thriving, encompassing that which we call life, trust provides the roots that we may grow tall, stand strong, and live our life convictions. Rooted in faith, rooted in God, we begin to shape our lives, our leaves green, and even flower at times. Yet fruit is not produced until these roots connect with another. This connection, this bond allows the roots to weave intermittently, for roots woven deep beyond the surface, which act as support for the living tree above. Grounded in trust, these roots, these braided roots, depend upon one another for nutrients to live, to thrive, to grow. Trusting, weaving, growing, giving—these are all braided in love and the byproduct is a fruit-bearing tree. *Trust*, a valued word, a complicated word, a word with such depth the only way to uncover its meaning is to look, look into the eyes of the beholder. Just see, feel, hear, know who, what looks back. I had learned how to trust, to let go of my ego and be the love that grew within me all because I took a moment to listen to my heart and accept my worth. Looking into the eyes of my best friend, I saw a pure heart looking back and her words penetrated my very being as she said, "You are love and worthy of the unconditional love you always speak about." How do you respond to such a poignant statement? Thus our faith journey developed, sharing faith, sharing our person. Step by step we walk, step by step we love, step by step we become ever entangled in faith dependent upon each other, dependent upon the love of God in our lives. True faith, coupled with a pure heart and beautiful soul creates a deep trust, a dependence unveiled in the eyes of a faithful companion. The discovery of such beauty within repurposes the soul and emancipates the heart. A soul now found, not by accident, but enveloped in unconditional love and protected in truth is a soul connected to another grounded in faith. A nonjudgmental forum in which the soul is encouraged to thrive, not just survive, develops over time, brought about by isolated victories and acceptance of self as seen through the eyes of an honored friend. TRUST- Timely real utterances of single truths. Initially met with trepidation but now embraced with love, peace, joy, and trust, for trust bolsters love, which unlocks the heart. The heart speaks the "wordless words" found in the depths of our souls, once too dark, too cavernous to explore for fear of what we might discover. Now with the companionship of a treasured friend, life is uncovered and celebrated, allowing us to move forward with a foundation of faith, a cornerstone of trust and abound in love.

Bounteous love, seemingly transitory in a reclusive society funneled by lies and deceit, is probable only when rooted in trust, offered with benevolence, and accepted in solace. Take for example the tiny sapling. A sapling stands tall reaching for the warm morning sun, yet its branches are barren, dwarfed and eclipsed by the mighty oak residing to its left. At first glance, it seems as though the sapling will not reap the rays of the sun and never reach its potential. Upon further investigation, it is made apparent that the mighty oak will not be the demise of the sapling but rather the cause of its success. The sapling is able to reap the nutrients from the sun without begin scorched by its direct rays. The mighty oak, which so lovingly shielded the young sapling from the fretful elements, still remains, branches intact, fully in bloom yet with a perplexing twist. The young sapling, now fully grown, has intertwined its branches among the mighty oak. They have become one entity, one beauteous, bountiful, flowering tree with two trunks. We are the young sapling attempting to grow, attempting to find our way in this world, often lurking in the shadows so as to become idle observers, not active participant who make mistakes. God is our mighty oak, residing by our side, bombarding us with grace and talents to flourish, to excel, to live our lives filled with faith, love, and fortitude.

A shield from the harsh rays of the sun, God often carries us through our roughest times yet even here we gain an understanding of self and learn how to put our best foot forward. Our branches grow, the trunk roots, leaves tickle the branches. Seasons pass, leaves fall, the barren branches are exposed to the cool winter air. Nothing penetrates the thick layer of ice that has formed on the branches during the cold winter months. Despair has overtaken the soul. Just when it seems that all hope is lost, the warm morning sun melts the ice and the sapling is able to feel again, able to breathe, and soak in the presence of God. Rejuvenated by the spring air, the sapling begins to grow into a mighty oak. Each leaf upon its branches serves as a reminder of the many gifts bestowed by God to withstand the pressures of life. Never alone, never abandoned, we have the courage to walk with God, fully aware of his presence in our lives. There will be times when the sun will become too much to bear and God will be our shield. Our mighty branches of faith, trust, and love become a safe haven in which the birds of the air will nest, squirrels will burrow, and young children will climb for a day of adventure. Unwilling to leave, for the view from the top is beautiful, young children will rest among our branches. We are safety, we are adventure, we are camouflage for our thick branches support the weight of the child and their burdens. Our intricate intertwining with the mighty oak brings forth images of pirate ships along the ocean, and the leaves are a blanket of warmth and the color of friendship. Our branches extended, we reach to the heavens, growing ever taller in faith and wider in love. A magnanimous image of grandeur and glory standing tall basking in the warm morning sun, we are this image. We are that breathtaking beauty. We are soaking in the warm morning sun—God within us. It is in our discovery of God within that we are

able to experience God abound, able to share God with others, and definitively choose our path in life. Choices are all around, each moment is a choice. Aware, we look, we feel, and we act.

Two sets of cards lie before us: pain coupled with self-loathing, conditional kindness, and unworthiness, or unconditional love embracing acceptance, understanding, and self-awareness. Which do we choose? Having operated with the first set of cards for so long, it is a difficult hand to fold. This bluff of a hand has taken its toll. No longer willing to be hurt, we must concede this game and start fresh with a new hand. We look at the goodness of God, we look at his love for us. We feel love even in the midst of turmoil and anguish, yet the other hand is still before us, untouched. *Change*, a negative word when uttered in any context, is the driving force of this game. It is much easier to do as we always did for, even in pain, it is familiar and for whatever reason familiarity equates comfort. *Novel*, foreign and different, incites fear in the hearts of many, but this is not the case to those people touched by the hand of God. The people of Israel proclaimed the greatness of God in songs of thanksgiving as they were led to safety from the grips of their enemies. This, a nation that God saved from total destruction. Surely, God will lead a loving, open heart to freedom. Their choice to pick up the cards of unconditional love, acceptance, understanding, and self-awareness come at a price. Yes, we have the opportunity to become our true self, reveling in the glory, which is God. Though the cards are placed before us they are difficult to pick up for a weight presses on us like a millstone around the neck. It is in our recognition of this weight and the need for help that we receive it in the form of a friend—a friend who picks up the cards and millstone and carries them until the load is able to be lightened enough for one person to carry. Stop and listen to the "wordless words" spoken by such a friend, the cards of change, the hand dealt, the burden lightened the load no longer cumbersome, for a friend intercedes. Listen, for the heart knows this friend. It has beckoned and prayed for such a person, the prayer answered with, "I am right here." I have been fortunate to have found a friend such as this, a person with whom I know I am safe, with whom I know I can be myself, the true unmasked self. Permitted to be me empowered me to always be me, no matter the situation. I now do not care what others think of me, I have learned to celebrate the God within me and celebrate I will.

With cards in hand, the game of life still poses a struggle. We live, we laugh, we love, we cry, we scream, and who hears? Life, a series of reactions to various circumstances, becomes a game well played when encapsulated in love, lived in faith, and encompassed in trust. Just when life seems to present a systematic, logical, yet unhappy flow, a blizzard hits, and we are left scrambling for things to help us weather this particular storm. In all the commotion, we notice a fellow shopper slowly walking each aisle of the market and carrying nontraditional storm items. Intrigued and bewildered with such a peaceful demeanor, we stop to engage in a conversation, ever guarded, thinking it may incite a heated argument for tensions in the market run high in the race against the impending storm. The stranger lovingly stops, and the conversation lasts for what seems like an hour. Parting ways, we cannot recall exactly what was discussed yet a feeling of peace and a sense of certainty fills our hearts. No longer frightened of the storm, we purchase our items and return home.

Home, a feeling of security, a feeling of love, a feeling of peace, a want, a hope to carry this with us always, not just in light of an epiphany.

Days later, we come across the same stranger who graciously set aside precious shopping time, and we engage in yet another conversation. Time passes, the stranger no longer a stranger but a confidant, a best friend, a spiritual soul mate. The unconditional love, unconditional acceptance, genuinely bestowed, establishes for us a safe haven in which to explore our soul, to unmask not only our emotionless face but unmask our hearts. With each mask that is peeled away, self-doubt and self-loathing initiates the return of the mask, yet it is the bombardment of love and acceptance from our very best friend that makes the unmasking process less frightening, less grueling. With the true self exposed, the walls once built as a protective and conforming mechanism begin to crumble. With no need to hide behind a stone wall, it begins to fall leaving us completely vulnerable with our imperfections real both to ourselves and to onlookers. The nakedness that would have previously paralyzed life is now embraced and feelings validated in the arms of a loving friend. Given permission to thrive, we set aside societal and secular norms for their encumbrances provide only survival. Now thriving under a blanket of love, acceptance, freedom, peace, and joy, an imminent storm stirs up only emotions of excitement. The home has been prepared for it is carried each day in the beauty of the soulful heart. So, at the onset of the storm, we find two friends drinking hot chocolate, nestled on the couch, engaged in prayer, enveloped in love, patiently awaiting the beauty of the new fallen snow.

When faith is shared, true friendship becomes the experience of a lifetime for words need not be exchanged as the heart has found its dwelling, it is home. No longer intimidated by the crass words of the mind, the heart is now free to live, to love, to seek, to find to explore the world all in light of acceptance, of truth, of God. Listen to the "wordless words" of the heart.

Journey to the heart, journey to the soul
The eyes hold the secret
When do we look, how do we know?
What truth is to be told
To me, the beholder?
God brings forth his beauty and glory
Demonstrated in the grandeur of you
I cherish your heart, your love, your soul
We speak without words for our souls connect
My eyes hold the key
To the lock on my heart
To set the soul free, to live, and to thrive
For in the depth of my heart, God speaks
He has give me a spirit, so free and so true
A connect, a knowledge personified in you
The truth that you hold
The safety you bring
Rejuvenates my hope, my faith, my spirit
I see with my eyes
The key thought lost
The key now found in the purest of hearts
You share with me
A valor of innocence
A splendor of joy
A persistence of assurance
My eyes wide to see
What my heart already knows

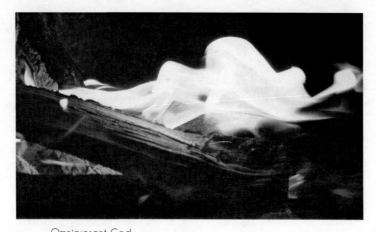

Omnipresent God
Unconditional friend
My blessing is twofold
For the dichotomy of intangible and tangible
Come alive in my life
My eyes reflect beauty
My heart lives the love
Shared by a best friend

Life is now complete, an enjoyable adventure, for it is lived in love, fortified in faith, and shared by a best friend. The most frightening experience is letting God in and living what the heart already knows, live the heart, live God.

FUTURE WAY

DESIRE PL

TRUST CIRCLE

Destined for Greatness

Destined for Greatness

Dreams, goals, desires—what do we seek? Most people would quickly answer health, wealth, and a thriving career. But what do we want to achieve? Who do we want to become? Who will we recognize in the reflection of the mirror when we are old? God has blessed each of us with unique gifts, yet it is up to us to unwrap and nurture these gifts. Even in our uniqueness, our charge is the same—to become the most complete, most splendid edition of us. Spiritual completeness, spiritual astuteness, spiritual awakening is that for which our hearts truly long. In our search for God, we discover love, humility, friendship, hope, and joy. These virtues, along with the guidance of the Holy Spirit, act as catalysts in our plight to uncover our most complete self. As children, we are constantly bombarded with the question, "What do you want to do in life?" Most children respond with, "I want to become a doctor, a veterinarian, or a CEO of a multimillion-dollar company." I believe we do a disservice to our children when we ask this question. Is that not just asking for a superficial, societal-forced answer? Instead, we should ask what desires lie within your heart?

I try to be cognizant of the questions I pose to my daughter as I don't want her to feel pressure to conform to conventional means of living. I continuously ask her, "How have you seen or hear God today?" One day I asked her what God looked like and she responded with, "Well, that is interesting. God is God; He just is." To which I responded, "Okay, then, what color does God feel like?" "Oh, that is much easier,

Mommy. God is every color of the rainbow because whatever mood I am in, God is right there with me."

Keep in mind my daughter is eight, but I was completely satisfied with the answer for it told me she had thought about God as a feeling and experienced God as a feeling. I smiled and hugged her and she went on be bopping around the house. Life is filled with choices from the clothes we wear to identifying the words of our heart. We can choose conformity or we can choose faith. Should we choose the latter, our posed questions must reflect the words of the heart. Sure, children could answer the same way, but if they understand that God is our soul, the answer to the posed question may be very different. For if we listen and honestly evaluate our individual talents and set our course to complete spiritual fulfillment, the result would be exponential joy.

Our sights are set, our destination is clear, and what is left? Determination, motivation, and prayer must be our driving force for the race has begun, and we do not want to be trampled in the herds of people racing to the finish line. Most people will never see the finish line for even the best intended miss a key factor in the accomplishment of goals. It is not the setting of goals that is difficult, for this idea is ingrained in us as young children. We know how to set our sights high, to want to win the biggest prize on the boardwalk. What we neglect to do is work to achieve them. Many people set magnificent goals only to wait, to live life in hopes of their dreams, yet they make no effort to make them come to fruition. I was one of these people, I wanted a faith-filled life yet I wanted it to come to me. I am a walking oxymoron for I spent hours upon hours in the gym working hard in the hopes to attain a scholarship to college. My hard work paid off, I became an Academic All-American and gained an education at the same time. The most

valuable lesson I learned while in college was that we make our own choices. Life is there for the taking but it is our awareness of our surroundings and our acceptance of self that permits us to drive as we have never driven. The same is true for our spiritual direction, though it is less attended to. We will spend hours on the court perfecting our shot but whine about an hour in the church pews. Somewhere along the line we fell into the trap that faith would just be handed to us. Yes, it is given to us without conditions but it is still up to us to open this gift and use it to its fullest potential. Each day I try to work on my spiritual gifts, my connections with God that I may share His inspired love with others. I dream, but now my dreams are in color, for no matter how I feel, God walks with me each step of the way. Yes, dreams, goals, desires burn within us. Yes, we have been blessed with the gift of faith. Yes, we are unique and therefore pursue different avenues. But the means to these avenues are the same: determination, motivation, faith, humility, and God. What have we perpetuated that our dreams may come true? The "wordless words" of the heart speak ever so clearly—love.

Ah, a tangled web we weave when filled with anxiety, doubt, and fear. Each strand a moment of doubt, a sigh of anxiety, a wince of fear. We become our own prey, tangled in the web, torment and discontent our predator. Suffocation the next step, negativity, and invalidated thoughts the weight. The pressure intensifies, the heart races, the mind analyzes with improper facts, the erroneous calamity our downfall. The heart is only permitted to feel what the mind thinks. As darkness closes in, the hope, thought to be abandoned, becomes the rallying force of the heart. The web hangs in the distance moving ever so slightly with the breeze. This could be the release desperately needed from the capture, but the wind is not strong enough for the entangling strands of silk. From the distance, a loving call is heard, yet with every pull and tug, the strands only tighten, solidifying our fate. Unable to speak for the devious predator has meticulously spun the web so as to imprison and to ensure its prey's entrapment. Moments pass, thoughts of defeat begin to set in, unseen stressors allow the mind to run rampant. We are unable to move, the predator ready to pounce. The voice heard in the distance is but a slight memory. Antagonizing, we wait—wait for what? What will be our fate? At the breaking point of despair, the voice is once again heard. This time, it is close. A rock cuts through the web like a knife through butter on a warm morning. We are free, and though the mind attempts to wander, the heart musters strength, courage, and faith, the world not so dark, not so frightening, the weight not so heavy, yet entrapment remains. It is the heart which takes the lead, the heart which does not fight what is seen as entrapments for it knows the strands, once deemed to us a prisoner, now enveloped in love. A web spun from anxiety, doubt, and fear morphs into a protective cocoon. Its encasing is love, solace, and hope. Nestled tight and secure in the cocoon, dubious thoughts are replaced with inundating feelings of love, of comfort, of protection. I will not become someone's prey, but I will continue to love and to be loved. The cocoon, my security blanket, allows me the freedom to be me without judgment, without conditions, without the threat of departure. The cocoon is warm, safe and I rest, I am calm. The heart has settled the mind for the mind now understands love.

Love, a grandiose word with magnanimous implications, acts as a bullet to the heart or a lifeline to the soul; the choice is ours. Modern culture associates the word "love" with a physical experience often reciprocated with "I will do for you if you do for me" attitude, which then subjugates feelings of love. Love dependent upon the actions of another is not love. Codependency is anything but love, for it fosters ill will and feelings of inadequacy. These misconstrued definitions of love eradicate the mere notion of true unconditional love as offered to us by God, let alone a trusted companion. We

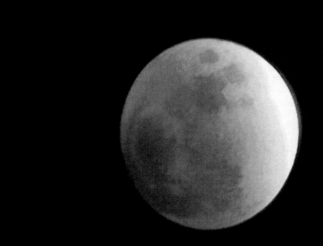

need to set aside these skewed definitions of love and turn to the truth of love, the truth of God, the truth of forgiveness, the truth of all that is unconditional. What lies before us, what lies beside us are nothing unless we understand and acknowledge that which lies within in us—love. God, friendship, acceptance, trust, faith—these are the semaphores of true love, true unconditional offerings of that which is heavenly, that which is perfected yet offered to us, imperfect models of love. God spoke to Abraham telling him that his descendants would be as numerous as the stars in the heavens. Too numerous to count, these same celestial lights are an offering to us as well. At first glance, the stars, seemingly luminous masses of plasma, illuminate the night making for casual conversations or romantic evenings. But to the trained eye, the luminous spheres offer much more; they are categorized energy sources permitting identification of patterns such as the little dipper that even an informed novice can readily identify. God's offering of love manifests itself ever so clearly in the person of Jesus. The image of the star over the manger, which led the wise men to the infant Jesus is just as powerful today as it was two thousand years ago. God constantly calls us and, if we choose to listen, His words are like lullabies to a troubled soul. A bright star shining for all the world to see is our lantern in the dark of the night. Just as the star's internal pressure prevents it from collapsing; our internal faith encased in love prevents us from despair. Love—the acceptance of imperfection, the acknowledgment of doubt, the surrender to forgiveness—coexists in the unconditional package of God.

God speaks with "wordless words," for he identifies us as love when he offers love. This, our unconditional gift if only we accept the offer.

Love
True, unconditional, pure
Brings to the surface sincerity, hope,
integrity, and truth
Thoughts with the heart
Thoughts with God

Love
Beautiful, quaint, whole
Permeates the heart, the world, our
lives
Thoughts of the heart
Thoughts of God

Love
Exciting, faithful, kind
Enveloped in wisdom, fortitude, and
understanding
Thoughts from the heart
Thoughts from God

Love
Novel, emotional, joyful
Hidden in sadness, fear, and hurt
Thoughts to the heart
Thoughts to God

Love
Peace, patience, holy
Thrives in freedom, trust, and promise
Thoughts concealed in the heart

Thoughts revealed in God

Love
Hope of tomorrow, promised yesterday, felt today
No conditions, free to be, free to live
Thoughts rooted in God
Manifested in friendship

Love
Unconditional, pure, true
Reminds me of a heart brought forth by light
Thoughts uncovered
Thoughts discovered

Love...

This is our offering, our promise from God, yet we often choose fabricated love which cuts, pains, and eradicates hopes and dreams. Mandates, expectations, and societal sanctions are thrust upon us imposing unrealistic margins of error, a.k.a. perfection. The existence of perfection is nothing more than a ruse which, when sought and unattained, leaves feelings of failure and defeat. Calloused and scarred, the mind takes control, once again seeking and longing for this phantasm of perfection. We go about life wanting what we want, and when we don't get it, we pout, we sulk, we complain, or we get loud and make a scene. These are falsehoods, ideals with which we base life. If we cannot see it, hear it, touch it, it is merely a mirage; its existence, a farce.

There is always hope in tomorrow, always hope in the complexity of change, always hope in the love God has offered. So tomorrow begins, a chance for change, a chance for acceptance, a chance for unconditional love. Each day begins anew, the sun rises, and with it is hope for the future, hope in our abilities, hope in what is to come. Hope is not enough to make the day rewarding. Hope is what allows us to rise in the morning, to get out of bed and tackle the day. Actions, strengthened by faith, engulfed in trust and surrendered to God, are what make the day successful, unique, and exciting. Thus, the day begins, and with it is our opportunity to become who we are, to find our strength and allow our actions to speak for themselves. God in our midst, God within our soul, God dwelling in our heart—do we carry God with us everywhere we go or does God carry us through life's journey? When we learn to trust, when we learn to hear, we know the presence of God in our lives. We learn to speak, we learn to listen, to act upon the call within our heart, the call to love, the call to be love, the call to live love. As the sun slowly rises high in the midday sky, so too our actions slowly rise to the call of God for righteousness commands a sense of duty, a sense of pride, a sense of understanding. The warmth of the sun's rays upon the earth mimics the warmth of God's love and compassion for us. His love encompasses all that we are, all that we desire to be, all that we know and we become safe to be that which we already are—us. Our prayers are heard, our doubts reconciled, our hopes alive all in the presence of God dwelling within our hearts. Protected and aware, we take action, and we live a God-centered life, and life becomes complete. We still struggle, we still stumble, we still fall, yet we have the strength to get back up, to not be embarrassed, to roll when we fall comes from that first sunrise, the sunrise of hope. Hope ignited the rays of light within our heart, yet actions permitted the fire to blaze. And when the sun slowly begins to set and we tire, when exhaustion of life

Colorful

Unique

Radiant

sets in, then God carries for his love is never ending. Rejuvenated in God's love, we are strengthened. We once again learn how to trust, learn how to live fully alive in God. As the night begins to fall and the day comes to a close, we are able to see in the darkness, for hope, the torch of the heart, will lead us through the dark, despairing nights to await with anticipation the morning sun. The day will begin anew, life awakened in the arms of God. And so we fall, fall into the arms of God that we may live.

God speaks, and the heart listens.

The beauty of You
Just as the sun rises each morning, the beauty of you shines upon those around you.
Warming them with your compassionate smile. You instill in others a sense of belonging, a sense of acceptance that can only come from a tender heart
This is your heart, tender and loving
Peace, joy, faith, self-worth
These our goals
Valiant efforts, striving for perfection
Perfection non-existent

Internal strife

Who am I?

Where do I fit?

Why am I?

These questions permeate our soul

We grumble and grip

We cry, and we scream

Tormenting our very being, our very soul, and we hurt

Masquerading this hurt, we forge on

Life becomes for us what others make of it

Free thought becomes enslaved to crippling criticism

Both from others and ourselves

This vicious cycle must be broken

Stop

Look

Listen with your heart

It speaks ever so gently, ever so softy, yet ever so truthfully

Peace, joy, faith, self-worth

These are at the core of our being

God resides within us

God presents us with a sublime present

The present of us

Yet society burrows this present

Among a heap of conformity, amid the longing for perfection

Dubious thoughts

Self-inflicted criticism and pain prevent us from unwrapping this gift

Non-existent perfection our wall

When hit, it hurts

Mistakes will be made

Sadness will penetrate our heart
Tears encapsulate our person
Trials and tribulations our life lesson
Hurt will no longer cripple
Tears wiped away
All with the unconditional love from
God
God within us
God around us
God loving us
We deserve love
We are love
The beauty of your heart
The temple of your soul

Allow it to reveal the beauty of you
Your eyes, the gateway to your tender heart
Look, see, its reflection is you.

We need to look at the love of God, look into the eyes of love, let go, and let the love of God penetrate our total being. Then, and only then, are we complete utterances of love able to share love and become love.

Bold Acceptance of the Wordless Words

Bold Acceptance of the Wordless Words

The essence of God is the breath of life, that which sustains, that which enlivens, that which gives spiritual life and, in turn, life itself. Defined by God, we are walking embodiments of grandeur, of hope, of love, of peace. Awakened, the spirit flows. It is free to breathe, free to reap the wonders of that which is before us, that which is discovered, hidden, buried for protective purposes. It is in its discovery that hope is ignited; it becomes the beacon in an otherwise dismal walk. Procurement of treasure the goal, the hunt is seemingly desperate, almost impossible for the treasure is feverishly buried in a moment of weakness, in a flash of doubt. Folklore paints a wondrous picture of this treasure, of the powers this treasure holds yet most never go in search for such treasure as it is too good to be true. Why waste time on a useless search? Reality is life, which is before us and therefore seen, heard, and felt. But there is one sense, the "God sense," which when used properly, becomes the guide to the beauty of life, the hope of the meaning of life, the reality of the purpose of life. The treasure, thought buried in the depths of the swamp, lies before us, lies within us waiting to be rediscovered. Today, the day of discovery, is the day life itself becomes the essence of God. Each breath taken is taken with purpose, each breath expelled is expelled with love. Life lived in love, in hope, is life lived in faith, in communion with God. Life's discovery comes at the very moment, the very second when the tides could have turned, when societal pressures could have ransacked life itself, yet the dwelling place of God is the essence of life. God dwells from within. It is in this discovery, this acknowledgement that we gain knowledge, we gain strength, and we gain the wisdom to breathe and become the essence of God.

A tiny dandelion is planted. Over time, it grows and sprouts into a pretty yellow flower—ordinary, yes—but colorful all the same. Time passes and the flower ages. The yellow is not as vibrant, and it begins to wither, or so it is thought. Soft white bristles replace the yellow flower. The night falls and morning follows, the "wish" flower now fully formed. The large white sphere stands tall among the crab grass, its flower soft and enticing. Young children gather to play and the "wish" flower is quickly snatched from the ground for the child believes the flower to be some sort of wish provider. With the last breath, she frees the soft white bristles that the wind may carry them through the air and find for them a new home. The now barren stem is tossed to the ground, and the child runs and plays, satisfied her "wish" flower will carry with it her innermost dreams and desires.

Funny, the ordinary dandelion, deemed a nuisance by most adults, quickly becomes a plaything to children. The white thistles silently carried through the air with the help of the child and wind allow the dandelion to once again take root and grow, this time in several places. We are that dandelion should we choose to free ourselves from our rational mind, from conforming to societal misconceptions as we listen and act upon God in our lives. Disguised as ordinary dandelions, we are able to grow and flower among the weeds, the hatred, the mistrust, the backstabbing that is society. And as the night closes in, we become transformed for warmth and love create a wholeness, a completeness. When the sun casts its light over the playground and the child picks that dandelion, it is not the end—rather, it is the beginning, for the dandelion is able to grow in many places.

As dandelions, we are able to grow in faith as the love of God penetrates our calloused hearts and they soften, not to the point of withering but to the point of life and thus are able to be shared. Just as the wind carries the soft thistle through the air and gently sets it down that it may take root, so too we live our faith that it may be shared and grow even deeper in the love of Christ. We need not fear turning from the yellow flower into the white "wish," for it is because of the latter that we are permitted and obligated to share our faith, our love, our God with others. It is in letting go of the encumbrances of the day that we begin to share the visions of God. My personal prayer is, "I am giving this to you God, placing it into your hands because I can no longer handle it." I have prayed this prayer many times but only a handful of times have I left my prayer with God. Most times I take it back for my ego wants fed, it wants reassurance of its effect on my life. It is in the times which I let the prayer go and surrender to God that I feel most alive, most complete for life is not to be lived in seclusion. Life is to be celebrated with each breath. Fear of change, fear of morphing into something other than the yellow flower will keep us living among the crabgrass. It is in sharing ourselves that we become who we are and we see our worth, our worth to God, our worth in God.

Worth identified, worth acknowledged, and life begins. Yet we are challenged to live life to the fullest, live it without regret. Regret only holds us back for we have become who we are at this moment in time by our choices of the past. In changing something from the past we only seek to change our person now. Without the heartache, I would not have sought love. Without the faith, I would not have identified the reality of God. Life does not come complete with an instruction manual, but it does come with a compass, a faith compass. It points north, for north is the inward bound direction of our heart. There will be times when we aimlessly wander life's trails, never forging new paths and life's gauge quickly empties. Drained of life energies, coasting already paved roads becomes a necessity. How do we refuel? How do we know when to go off road or maintain our course?

John Lennon once said, "Life is what happens when you are busy making other plans." I can attest that life happened to me while I was busy planning my life instead of living my life. God does not intend for life to *happen*. The happenings of life will not cause joy, peace, or fulfillment. The effort put forth into any project, any situation, any aspect of life is directly proportional to the return. So it becomes our decision to refuel, to check our gauges and keep them where they need to be. Whether we sink or swim, skate by on good looks, or head full force into our future, the decision lies within our person. This need not lie upon our shoulders like a heavy weight restricting our breathing. Laborious thoughts need not consume. They need not become so cumbersome and awkward that life becomes unsteady, uncertain, and we surrender just so as to not drown. Life's outlook, the route chosen on this roadmap of sanity becomes much more visible when trust navigates, not just the detours with bouts of sanity. Knowing God offers nothing but love, tenderness, comfort, and support is like knowing how to change a spare tire. The journey becomes less fearful because even a flat tire in the middle of the desert becomes a mere happenstance. But when you find a kindred spirit, one who is an extension of yourself, one with whom you can share thoughts—good, bad, indifferent—life takes a new course. Life does not just happen, paved roads are never seen again and the adventure, though just begun, is complete. Refueling becomes a thing of the past for the gauges never move, the connective energy recharges as love is shared, as trust is shared, as peace is found. God gently speaks and the heart listens, the heart guides and the spirit is filled, it leaps with joy while it rests in peace, for love abounds in a journey set forth in trust. New paths are explored yet trepidation is a notion of the past for God is found, God is celebrated not by one but by two. Let the journey of a lifetime, for a lifetime, begin for love will never tease, hope will never torment, trust will never waver, God will continue to speak, the heart will listen, and peace will be the destination sought and found at each rest stop along the journey. Destination set, car prepared, mind at ease, heart the guide, course not mapped. In fact, no map is packed for the heart knows the way, the heart knows the sound of God's voice and will follow accordingly. God's voice speaks to a kindred spirit and the road becomes exciting yet calm, the journey an adventure, one which we are fully equipped to handle.

Still with acceptance, there comes doubt, for the road will be rocky, the bumps will cause discomfort, and the mind will wander impeding upon the actions of the heart. Questions will begin to circumvent the spirit. What if red were blue and blue were green? Logic would be disconnected, discounted, for proofs nonexistent, theorems mistrusted. Rationale would be laughed at, mocked. Life, as we know it, would be forever altered as would our course of action. The roads once taken would no longer exist, paths grown over, only thickets and weeds remain. With no roads nor paths, we would assume life to be chaos, even possible anarchy, yet it is anything but chaotic. Life, when led by the heart, is placid, joyful, and harmonious. The heart, the dwelling place of God, finds a way to gently guide our life, without force, without constrictions yet with consequences of love, of fulfillment, of completeness. Finding our worth, finding that which we deserve, the unconditional love, unconditional forgiveness, the unconditional everything God has to offer becomes real, it is fully comprehended and accepted. Life is lived for life is love, and treasures are discovered and celebrated; hence, our worthiness is uncontested. God's world, shunned by most, is like the most perfect playground of a child. Free will is not inhibited by freedom, freedom is promulgated by worthiness, and worthiness is incited by unattached promises. Truly alive, our heart, mind, and body work as one entity, for they are one, and the product is harmony, joy, and peace. Expressions of faith, daring to relax in the arms of God, inviting God to lead us through life's crooked paths, calling upon God to fulfill his promise of love, we see life no longer as series of "have to's" but of "want to's." It is in these offerings of self to God that our world doubles in size for our eyes are opened for the first time to see that which God sees, we are able to feel that which God feels, we are able to know that which God knows—*love*.

Abandon the wreckage of the mind and

enjoy the love of the heart!

Voids filled, wreckage abandoned, the demons of our mind, our logic all cast out like demons haunting, tormenting our soul. With eyes closed, heart open, and mind tempered, we embrace the world of God, and we experience love for the first time, for peace is the song in the air and joy the dance. God calls, we hear, we acknowledge, and we walk into a world devoid of rationale but saturated in truth. Love is truth, and truth is God; therefore, God is love, and truth is love. Embracing such love, such truth, embracing God we discover life, freedom, and harmony. Embrace, discover, live, love. Your choice, your life, you are love.

Left Fielder's Prayer

Left Fielder's Prayer

In our acceptance of love, of faith, of trust, of God, we are often left with feelings of being different, in some ways alienated from others around us. While these feeling are unconfirmed, nonetheless, they linger and cause anxiety. We are not alone, we need only to open our hearts and connect with God, connect with those who live their faith. We need to share faith, and we will feel love. Until then, here is my prayer for those who feel like they are in left field...

So far in left field, many don't even know it is being covered. Those who look to left field see a speck and worry if the fly ball will be caught. When it is, they come to depend upon a shoestring catch for the final out. But that left fielder can't relate to the rest of the team no matter how hard they try; for year after year, left field is played deeper and deeper, making signals difficult to comprehend. Coming to bat every once in a while makes for a nice break in the monotony. But once three outs are made, the trek back to left field is often lonely, for the brief socialization acts as a tease. The silence in left field is deafening, out of range to communicate with the team and spectators. Introspection becomes a time-filler between pitches. This game is unlike any other game; during the seventh inning stretch, left field became a place of interest. Some even visited left field to get a feel for the surroundings, conversations we enjoyed, catch was even played, but alas, the game resumed, and players returned to their positions. A team consists of nine players working as one, each cognizant of their role and their efforts to win the game. This left fielder's job is to guard left field that on the off chance that the ball is pulled, the out attained. And so the "wordless words" again spoken, bent in prayer, the heart speaks, and God listens: God, grant me the foresight to see the pull of the bat that I may always be in position to protect my field. I make no qualms about my importance to the team for my fight for position was painstakingly grueling yet rewarding. Here, your presence settles my fears, tempers my anxiety, and yet excites my soul while opening my heart. I see you with my heart, I feel your gentle touch with every ounce of my being, and I know your unconditional love as it overwhelms my every move. You have brought me here to learn, to hear, to grow in truth, trust and joy. It is here I find the grass is greener as you embody all that is good, all that is right, all that is felt. Emotions overtake me. I am complete for I feel love, joy, peace, solace, and tranquility permeate my soul as I become relaxed in your arms. While I am not isolated from pain, hurt, or heartache, I am shielded by your omnipresent promise in my life. Your wisdom is my guide, your acceptance my fortress, your love my strength to continue the game in any kind of weather. Fortitude enables me to make the diving catch when necessary, for I am empowered to cultivate my faith, through feelings and belief in the truth of the story dwelling within my heart—the story narrated by you. I have come to learn how to listen, how to hear your call in my life. As with the crack of the bat, I move with anticipation for the fly ball. It is with every feeling that overtakes me that I long to become closer to you. Moving forward in our relationship, I learn to trust, to share, to experience you in all that I do, say, think, feel, and hear. While most begrudgingly make the trek to left field, I run with pride to cover this position for the knowledge I have gained while in left field has set my soul on fire and I have become alive with your spirit. I pray that this game never ends, that the pitcher never tires, so my faith may mature and my heart awaken to your gentle call of love. Amen.

Though we may, at times, feel alone in this world devoid of morals, we are never alone. Though we may feel like an outcast when we show kindness, when we live our faith, we are not alone for God strengthens each step. We may feel like a lonely left fielder, but we need to remember there are thousands of games played each day with thousands of left fielders covering the field. We are not alone, faith our bond. Discover your faith, discover God, just look within. Your discovery will be the discovery of a lifetime for it will be the discovery of life itself!

Is the constant noise of your mind drowning out the gentle call of God to your heart? Are you trapped in constant cycles of worry, panic, fear, regret, doubt, and anxiety? You are not alone.

The human mind is a valve that can filter out the loving call of God. Over time, your mind will trick you into believing that God's unconditional love is not possible for you. In *The Land the Mind Forgot*, you will learn how to turn down the blaring volume of the mind and turn up the call of God's love in your heart. You will read passages that allow you to venture beyond your mind to the depths of your heart and soul and discover that true peace, genuine love and sustaining joy can be yours.

Set aside your worries and fears and journey to *The Land the Mind Forgot* where you can connect with a God who loves and accepts you unconditionally. Your acceptance of this love will transform your life and the lives of those around you. Adventures of the heart await you. Let go of the mind and listen.

DANIELLE FIORINI has a Theology degree with a specialization in Education. She has taught morality and theology for ten years and was a camp director for fifteen years. Her expertise is in relating to children, especially teenagers, and teaching them about God's unconditional love. Her family is the source of her inspiration.